TIM PRITCHARD

street boys

7 kids. 1 estate. No way out.
The true story of a lost childhood.

I'd like to thank Natalie Jerome for her enthusiastic and insightful support for this project, Sara Fisher for her advice and encouragement and my family and friends for their continued love and support. Sgt Toby McDaniel of the Metropolitan Police, Earl Myers at the Angell Town recording studio and Roger Samuels provided invaluable insights into the PDC and their life on the estate. Above all I'd like to thank Sharon Kerr and all those in the PDC for sharing their stories with me.

In order to protect privacy, some names, identifying characteristics, dialogue and details have been changed or reconstructed.

HarperElement
An Imprint of HarperCollins*Publishers*
77–85 Fulham Palace Road,
Hammersmith, London W6 8JB

www.harpercollins.co.uk

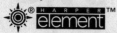

and HarperElement are trademarks of HarperCollins*Publishers* Ltd

First published by HarperElement 2008
This edition 2008

5

Extract from 'Electric Avenue' by Eddie Grant
used by permission of Warner/Chappell Music.

A catalogue record of this book is available from the British Library

ISBN-13   978-0-00-726706-4
ISBN-10   0-00-726706-1

Printed and bound in Great Britain by
Clays Ltd, St Ives plc

Mixed Sources
Product group from well-managed
forests and other controlled sources
www.fsc.org   Cert no. SW-COC-1806
© 1996 Forest Stewardship Council

FSC is a non-profit international organization established to promote the responsible management of the world's forests. Products carrying the FSC label are independently certified to assure consumers that they come from forests that are managed to meet the social, economic and ecological needs of present and future generations.

Find out more about HarperCollins and the environment at
www.harpercollins.co.uk/green

Preface

Everyone was out there and there were gunshots.
Bang, bang, bang, bang. Young kids crying, everyone was
scattering. It was hectic. Someone had been shot. I didn't
know the guy. We were all young. There was blood
everywhere, man. The guy'd been shot in the face.

Inch

This is the story of JaJa, Phat Si, Inch, Birdie, Ribz, Bloods and Tempman. They are members of the PDC, one of the most feared and notorious street gangs in London. To some they are glamorous, gun-toting 'gangstas', with a bling-bling lifestyle. To others they are a group of criminal thugs who pose a danger to civilized society. This may turn you on, or it might put you off. But stay with it. Things may not be what they seem.

Tim Pritchard

Foreword

by Elijah Kerr (aka JaJa)

This book is the voice of the streets. An unheard voice.

This is what happens when you leave those voices unheard, when you leave kids out there with no help and no support, and no choices or nothing.

This is what happens.

Your kids could be me. Your kids could go through the same things that I went through. I want you to understand what is out there, what young people like me are going through and why we are doing it.

It's a big cry for help, now.

Seven Kids

JaJa, real name: Elijah Kerr
Born in Birmingham and arrives in Angell Town at the age of ten

Phat Si, real name: Simon Maitland
Born on the Stockwell Park Estate, across the road from Angell Town

Bloods
Born in Kingston, Jamaica, and arrives in Angell Town at the age of six

Inch, real name: Nathan Cross
Born in Angell Town

Birdie, real name: Michael Deans
Born in Angell Town

Ribz, real name: Byron Cole
Born in Stockwell, down the road from Angell Town. Moves to Angell Town at the age of nine

Tempman, real name: Darren Samuels
Born in Tulse Hill, just up the road from Angell Town

Chapter One

The Raid

Could I have gone through a different door? If I'd been told to be a plumber and could have made money, maybe I would have gone down that route. Or if I'd met a fireman first or been shown some other life maybe I wouldn't be here now. But no one in the 'hood does those types of things. The people I met in Angell Town were drug dealers and burglars. That's what I knew first. There's not really no choice.

JaJa

It was Naja who first noticed that something was up. He saw a white police van reverse into the estate and then quickly drive out again. He didn't quite know why but something told him that it might be a police dog unit. He looked around nervously at the others.

'Something dodgy is going on.'

The others hadn't seen it. Ribz, who had already been there for an hour, was smoking weed and 'coching', Angell Town speak for chilling.

'Relax, Naj. It's cool.'

Naja wasn't so sure.

There were only five of them on the Marston House walkway that day. On any other day there would be eight or nine of them, but JaJa, Naja's older brother, had gone off to Wandsworth prison to visit Blacker who was serving time, Birdie had taken off a couple of hours earlier and Phat Si was on Brixton Road buying some takeaway jerk chicken. That left Naja, Ribz, Inch, Sykes and Skippy pacing the council block's second-floor corridor armed with small plastic bags of weed and heroin. They were waiting for the first 'cats', or punters, to arrive.

It was Tuesday 17 December 2002 at about 3 p.m. and it was bitterly cold.

None of them had any real reason to be alarmed. From their position on the second-floor walkway of Marston House they had a clear view over the whole estate. They would have plenty of warning if the 'feds' came. That's what they called the police, a name taken from all the American gangster shows they'd watched on TV. And anyway, they were sure that most of the residents would tip them off if there were any signs of police activity. Even though what they were doing was illegal, they were still surrounded by friends and neighbours. All of the gang had grown up in Angell Town. Ever since they were tiny kids, they'd ridden their bikes, kicked a ball about and run around in the streets and concrete playground at the heart of Angell Town. JaJa and his younger brother Naja had even grown up in one of the flats in Marston House, just along the corridor from where they were now standing.

When it was built in the 1970s, Marston House was designed

as a model of urban planning. Now the ugly, squat, concrete council block with its urine-stained and graffitied stairwells was mostly empty and derelict, earmarked for demolition as part of Lambeth Council's scheme to regenerate the area. It was still the centre of their world, though. 'The block' was their fiefdom. Here they ruled the roost as the most feared or, depending on your allegiance, the most respected gang in the area. Their name, the PDC, the Peel Dem Crew, was taken from 'peel dem', Jamaican street slang for 'rip them off', 'steal from them'.

And they had done plenty of that. They had all served time in young offenders' institutions and prisons for muggings, armed robberies, gun crimes and 'steaming'. It had been all the craze a couple of years earlier. A bunch of them would charge into a shop, such as a newsagent's, a supermarket, or even a bank or building society, and just go for the till and take whatever they could. Often the shopkeepers or bank clerks had no time to react. Or if they did, the gang would just run them over and knock them to the ground. They'd have raided the till before anyone could raise the alarm.

From below came the sound of shouting. *Something is about to go down.* This time Naja kept the thought to himself. He stamped his feet to keep warm.

'Go and find out what is going on.'

Inch was closest to the stairwell. He headed along the landing towards the stairs. He was small and stocky. That's how he got his street name. He was sure that it was just some of the 'cats' causing a commotion. He suspected that there was another gang nearby trying to muscle in on the action by stirring up the punters to take their custom away from the PDC.

Too much noise was never good for business. On a good day they could each make several hundred pounds, but some days the punters just didn't show up and they were left with unsold bags of weed or wraps of 'B' and rocks of crack cocaine. Those were the days when 'shotting', as they called it, felt like hard, boring and cold work. The laws of supply and demand for 'B' or 'Brown', more commonly known as heroin, were the hardest to predict. The customers for heroin tended to be real addicts who turned up at any time of the day or night demanding their fix. The money they used to buy the brown powder was always 'dirty' money, stolen generally, perhaps from a mugging that might have happened just a few hours previously. All the gang recognized that with addicts you could never be sure where the money came from. It came from 'God knows where'. But as long as they got the cash they didn't mind. The addicts preferred to operate in the shadows. That's why Inch had to get the commotion sorted out. If necessary he could get hold of some pistols or a MAC 10 sub-machine gun stashed away with friends, but he didn't believe it would come to that.

He headed down the stairwell of Marston House and got a waft of the familiar, bitter smell of dank concrete impregnated with ammonia and disinfectant. He was going to tell whoever it was to go away and that they didn't want them standing around there. *I'm going to tell them to breeze.*

Above him, on the second-floor walkway, Ribz leaned against the wall and drew on a joint. He felt chilled and temporarily released from his main preoccupation. Recently he'd tried again to find out more about his dad whom he hadn't seen since he was five years old. He'd heard that he was in America. Several years ago, when he'd visited his mum in prison, she had told him that his dad had fathered lots of children by different women and consequently Ribz had unknown numbers of brothers and sisters living on the estate. A constant anxiety of his when he was chatting up some girl was that she might be his sister. It was something he tried not to think about.

A car drove past, blasting out the beat of Sean Paul's latest dance hall reggae hit, 'Gimme the Light'.

Suddenly there were two loud bangs and an explosion of raucous yelling. Naja and Skippy looked round to see undercover cops appearing out of doors at either end of the block. Four cops were running towards them shouting and screaming.

'Don't move. Don't move. Police.'

Naja was stunned. He was caught on both sides. Two of the cops jumped on him, pushed him against a wall and jerked his hands up behind his back. Sykes was thrown to the ground.

Ribz tried to run but was immediately surrounded. One of the cops grabbed him by the throat, hauled him along the block and pushed him to the floor. Ribz fell on his chest. He felt all the air being squeezed from his lungs and everything went black.

Skippy was pushed to the ground, a knee pressed into the small of his back, his arms yanked behind him and his wrists snapped into cuffs.

Inch was half way down the stairwell when he heard the shouts and the cries on the landing behind him.

'Stay where you are.'

He saw everybody running in different directions. He didn't stop to think. He blasted down the stairs and out into the road and just kept running. Out of doors and alleyways more plain-clothed and uniformed police appeared, but Inch wasn't pulled over. He hurdled a police car and sprinted along Overton Road and disappeared out of Angell Town onto Brixton Road. He hardly noticed Phat Si walking towards him.

Phat Si was ambling back across Brixton Road towards Marston House carrying some takeaway jerk chicken for Inch when he got a call on his mobile phone that there was a dog unit hanging around Angell Town. He turned into the estate and saw the amazing sight of Inch sprinting away from Marston House chased by a posse of policemen. Phat Si stopped and watched in astonishment as Inch leapt over a police car and disappeared through an alleyway out of the estate with the group of desperate policemen pounding after him.

That's when Phat Si realized how institutionalized he'd become. He was slow. He was so stuck on his feet. Nearly ten years of prison and young offenders' institutions as well as the mind-numbing effects of years of drug taking had caught up with him.

He carried on walking up the road towards Marston House, his mind in such a daze that he nearly knocked over Pastor Samuels, Angell Town's feared but respected Christian preacher, who was returning home with bags of shopping.

'Simon. I wouldn't go up there. The police are arresting all the kids.'

Phat Si nodded but didn't stop.

'Listen. Don't get involved with what's happening. Stay here with me. The police will get you too.'

Phat Si didn't listen. It had been a long time since he'd listened to anybody. Ever since he was eight years old he had done just as he liked. That's how old he'd been when his mum had walked out on him, leaving him in the care of a father who was rarely there. Since then the only person Phat Si listened to was Phat Si.

Even though the streets now seemed to be howling with the sound of police dogs and police sirens, he continued walking through the police cars and police cordons right up to Marston House. He climbed the stairs and emerged on the landing to discover his friends were getting handcuffed and twisted up. In his best voice he approached one of the cops.

'What's going on, officer?'

'Go away.'

'What do you mean go away? You go away.'

'Just fuck off right now. Fuck off.'

Phat Si looked down on the ground to see one of his posse squirming under the grip of a hefty plain-clothed cop. Skippy was looking up at him, half mouthing, half whispering at him.

'Blow, you dummy, blow.'

But Phat Si didn't get out of there. Instead he looked down from the balcony at the commotion below. A policeman looked up, saw him and then looked at his colleague as if to say 'You fucking idiot.' That's when both of them got up and ran for Phat Si. Phat Si was so slow that he had hardly moved before they jumped on him.

When Ribz came to he found himself sitting on the stairs, hands in cuffs with a sergeant yelling in his face.

He'd been out of it for about five minutes. Ribz still didn't understand what was going on.

'Look, I ain't done nothin'.'

'Shut it.'

'What's going on? Why are you holding my neck?'

'The chief is coming down, he'll explain to you.'

A cop was yelling in his face.

'We saw you throw twenty rocks over the balcony.'

'They never came out of my pocket.'

Another cop arrived.

'It was you. I saw you. It was you.'

Ribz, Naja, Sykes and Skippy sat on the floor, dazed and handcuffed. It was as though the cops had come out of the doors and windows of every empty flat on the second floor of Marston House.

Neighbours were now congregating at windows and doorways watching the running battle. Chantelle, JaJa and Naja's sister, came out of 124 Marston House, only ten doors down from where the PDC were getting handcuffed. She had heard the shouting and screaming and seen the police running up to the second-floor landing and grab her younger brother Naja.

Now she came out of the flat ready to 'give the feds hell.'

She ran up to the policeman holding Naja and shouted in his face.

'What's he done? He wasn't doin' nufin'. He was just standing on the block.'

'He was caught selling drugs. Now go away before I arrest you too.'

Chantelle just stood there shouting at the policeman, telling him to let her little brother go.

JaJa had left Wandsworth prison and was on his way back to Angell Town to meet the others. He was just congratulating himself that he wasn't doing the drug selling shift at Marston House on such a cold day when he got a call from his mother.

'The police have raided Marston House. They've taken Naja.' She sounded frantic.

JaJa ran home. Naja was his younger brother and for years, ever since they were tiny kids, JaJa had been given the task of looking after him. His father had beaten up his mother and to stay alive she'd had to take her kids away from the family home. Since then, JaJa had taken the role of the man in the house and, although he'd been in and out of prison, he was expected to keep his younger brother out of trouble.

That's why, when JaJa got home, his mother was furious with him.

'They've taken Naja to Brixton police station. It's your fault. You're supposed to be looking after him.'

JaJa tried to remain calm. He knew that when he'd left the other members of the PDC earlier that day at Marston House none of them had any guns on them and the amount of gear they had could be passed off as drugs for their own use. He wasn't worried. He believed they'd all be able to get off.

The doorbell rang. JaJa went to answer it. Standing in the hallway were three police officers.

'Elijah Kerr. We are arresting you on suspicion of supplying class A drugs.'

JaJa wasn't worried. *I don't have any drugs on me. I don't have any in the flat. They can't get me for nothing.* He treated the whole thing like a joke.

'I've done nufin' wrong. You can't pin anything on me.'

'That's what you think.'

'Shut it. You've got nufin' on me.'

The policemen just laughed in his face and took him away.

When he got to Brixton police station the others, including Naja, Phat Si, Ribz, Skippy and Sykes, were all there, being held in separate cells. The police were still laughing and joking around.

JaJa shouted at the others through the cell bars.

'We're goin' home, don't worry, man. They ain't got nufin' on us.'

But no matter how much confidence he showed, how chilled he felt, the policemen around him still seemed to react with delight whenever he protested that they were clean.

Locked in their cells, JaJa and the others banged on pipes and yelled at each other through the bars, in a potent mixture of excitement and trepidation.

'We'll be out of here soon.'

The police yelled back telling them to shut up.

Late that night they took JaJa into an interview room. He knew what was going on. He'd been through the same process many times before. He wasn't worried. But when he saw the TV screen and the video camera he knew something bad was about to go down.

The investigating officer pulled out a small videotape and put it in the camcorder. He turned on the television. JaJa looked on in amazement as the screen flickered into life to reveal a shot of the balcony of Marston House. It showed figures walking up and down the second-floor landing handing over small bags and collecting money from punters. The tapes went back a whole month. JaJa cursed himself. He'd felt that something had been up for several weeks but he'd never reacted to it properly. He now realized that the police had inserted undercover surveillance teams into the empty flats in Marston House and its neighbouring blocks and had secretly videotaped them for weeks. JaJa had the sort of flash of insight that only occurs under extreme pressure.

That's money for you. It's the risk. It makes you do stupid things. Sometimes when you're on the street you need it so much it blinds you. Even from obvious things.

When Ribz was taken into the interview room and shown the same videotapes he protested. The tapes they had on him only showed him walking up and down the stairs in Marston House. They didn't show him actually selling drugs. But the cops had a surprise for him. When they tested his fingers they were stained with a special ink. Undercover officers had bought drugs from him using marked notes. Ribz knew then that he would have to admit his guilt. *I'm bang to rights.*

Back in his cell JaJa thought about the effect it would have on the others. It was Phat Si he felt most sorry for. Naja, Sykes and Ribz were young offenders so they'd probably get a year in some young offenders' institution. Skippy had only ever received minor convictions. JaJa had managed to stay out of prison for a couple of years so the court might be lenient on him. But Phat Si had just come out of a long prison sentence. He'd been suspected of attempted murder but, in the end, was found guilty of firing a gun into a crowd. He'd only been out a matter of weeks and now he was going back in again. The only good thing was that somehow Inch had slipped the police net.

* * *

As soon as he'd got out of Angell Town and onto the Brixton Road after the police raid, Inch knew that he was on the run and he wasn't sure where it would end. From Brixton Road he fled to his girl's place. He had to avoid the 'feds'. He was panicking. *Fucking hell. At least JaJa isn't nicked. That makes it better.* He had no idea that, at that very moment, JaJa was also being led in handcuffs to Brixton police station. He didn't tell his girlfriend what was going on but he knew that she realized that something was up.

> *She could see the way I was and I knew I can't get nicked*
> *but I was stuck and I couldn't think properly, innit? It was*
> *crazy, man. I was thinking of getting out of the country. I*
> *was dumb, I should have breezed but I was too scared. I*
> *thought no way am I going to the airport. What if they nick*
> *me there? I'll be mad.*

Inch called some of his friends, who told him not to worry and tried to calm him down. He decided then that he would hang out and stay with friends in different places. That way he would never be in one place for too long. That way the police wouldn't be able to track him down.

It would be two months before he was caught.

A month after the Marston House raid, Ribz, Sykes and Naja were taken to the Inner London Crown Court in Camberwell and sentenced, under their real names, Byron Cole, aged 19, Michael Payne, aged 21 and Naja Kerr, aged 18, to twenty-one months in Feltham. Later that same day, Skippy aka Errol Cole, aged 23, was given three and a half years. Phat Si and JaJa, real names, Simon Maitland and Elijah Kerr, both aged 22, got three years and nine months.

By the time he got out two years later, Elijah Kerr, aka JaJa, was a changed man. But the world outside had also changed. Marston House, the council block he'd grown up in, had been demolished to make way for brand new, award-winning housing. The Angell Town estate had been redeveloped. Brixton had been yuppified. Britain had gone to war in Iraq.

Within three months of his release, JaJa's fellow PDC gang members Blacker, Ham and Justyn would be gunned down in the streets around Brixton. Phat Si would be shot in the leg outside JaJa's flat. A new, radical Islam would be preached on the streets outside JaJa's local mosques in Stockwell and Brixton. Four suicide bombers would kill scores of people in the heart of London. An innocent Brazilian would be shot in the head at the local tube station. Things were changing, and changing fast.

Chapter Two

Elijah

I often wonder whether it would have been different. If I hadn't been abused and beaten by my partner. If I hadn't taken them out of their school and if we'd stayed in Birmingham, I wonder whether Elijah would have turned out different.

Sharon Kerr

JaJa's dreadlocks: that's what first got him into trouble. His father was a Rastafarian and as soon as JaJa's hair was long enough he wore it in ever-expanding knots of matted hair. It was fine at home where his two younger sisters, his younger brother Naja and his mother and father also wore dreadlocks, but at school there was one kid who kept pulling his hair during fights in the playground. It made JaJa fight even more furiously and soon got him into trouble with the school authorities. One evening, when he was seven years old, he went back to his small family home at 97 Crompton Road in Handsworth, Birmingham, ready for a confrontation.

JaJa's mum was in the kitchen. He told her that he wanted to have normal hair like other kids. They argued about it all night, but the next day she relented and took JaJa to have his dreads cut off. He knew she didn't approve of his request because she kept calling him 'Elijah'. That was his real name: Elijah Kerr, born in 1979 at Dudley Royal Hospital in Birmingham to parents who had left Jamaica as kids to start a new life in England. Most people, though, except schoolteachers and angry parents, just called him JaJa.

JaJa's parents, Sharon and Delroy, had met when they were young, during their third year at school in Birmingham. They started off just hanging around together as friends but it wasn't long before they started going out as boyfriend and girlfriend. The trouble was their relationship didn't go down well with either set of parents. Delroy's parents objected because they didn't want him to be distracted from his ambition of joining the army. Sharon's parents objected because Delroy was a Rasta. In the end, all it did was throw Sharon and Delroy even closer together.

When Sharon became pregnant at 14, it was Delroy's mum who took control. She grabbed Delroy by the arm and took him round to see Sharon's parents.

When everyone was sitting down she came straight to the point.

'Sharon's pregnant and Delroy's the father. What shall we do about it?'

Sharon's dad couldn't believe it. When Delroy and his mum had gone he glared accusingly at his wife.

'This is all your fault.'

Then he started slapping his wife around the face.

'I won't have a daughter like that living under my roof.'

It was too much for Sharon. The worst thing was seeing her mum submit to the beating. Sharon decided to act. She went upstairs, packed a suitcase, walked out of the family home and never went back.

Sharon moved straight into a squat with Delroy. It was a struggle at first, but her mum used to come round and sneak £10 notes to her without her father noticing. It was only when Elijah was born that her father started to pay any attention to her. Before that, her father had always treated her as the black sheep of the family. Elijah was his first grandson and he started to come round more often, but by then, for Sharon, it was too late.

Sharon and Delroy had their second child, Chantelle, and moved into a house in Crompton Road, Handsworth. They were cosy together and Delroy got work on various building sites. He was a strict vegetarian and cooked delicious dinners for her and the kids. A third child, Saffiya, was born. Every evening they would sit down together over a steaming hot meal of fish and rice and he would tell her all about Rasta culture and her roots in Africa. For Sharon it was an eye-opener. No one had ever told her about slavery, about Africa, about where she came from. For the first time in her life she felt that she was part of a proper family.

But then it started to go wrong. Delroy mentioned a building project he'd been offered in Africa. He began to disappear for weeks on end. Their fourth child, Naja, was born. Then one day Delroy announced he'd signed up for a short contract job in Ghana.

'I'll be back in six months.'

It was two years before he returned.

JaJa wasn't quite sure exactly when he noticed that his dad stopped being around. The biggest sign was when the music on the stereo changed. It had always been a familiar voice that floated down the street as he made his way home after school.

'Let's get together and feel all right…'

Bob Marley or some other mellow reggae artist was his father's music of choice, but lately as his absences became more frequent it was Roberta Flack or Marvin Gaye who greeted him. That was the music his mother liked. One day, out of the blue, his mum told him that his dad had gone to work in Africa, in Ghana, labouring on a building site or some sort of construction project. JaJa had the feeling that there was more to it than that but he didn't know what it was. But the longer his father stayed away, the more it became some sort of family secret that no one mentioned.

Anyway, his dad never wrote to him and soon it was as though he had been away forever. From then on Elijah didn't even miss him that much. He was close to his mum, though. His mum was like a sister to him. She'd got pregnant with him when she was only 14 years old and the bond was tight. From a young age he recognized how difficult it was for her to bring up four kids alone. He did his best to help out by giving the younger kids their cornflakes in the morning, getting them ready for school and packing their lunch boxes with sandwiches, crisps and chocolate bars.

Then, one morning, when he was eight years old, his dad suddenly reappeared. JaJa woke up and there he was, standing at the foot of the bed. He recognized him straightaway even though the long dreadlocks he'd had before he went away were now cut short. He ruffled their hair and gave them each a hug.

'You grown big, you're getting big now.'

He started to tell them a story about being in Africa and that he was on a construction project building a house. He said how he was on the beach and how he got his leg caught in seaweed and how it pulled him under and he nearly drowned. The best bit though was when he gave them presents: T-shirts, ornaments and African wooden carvings. The carvings were of ugly faces. They laughed and joked over the funny wooden faces. They each got a sugarcane stick to suck on. It was a laugh having his dad back.

The good times didn't last. His dad became moody. Then the beatings started. It was true that JaJa was the sort of kid who often got up to mischief. He was always out and about and things would sometimes just happen. Things would get broken. People would get upset with him. It started with a few lashes of his dad's belt. But one day his father really lost it. He ran upstairs to JaJa's bedroom and started hitting him with anything he could lay his hands on.

He gave me a beating that has always stuck in my head. Not because of the beating itself but because he beat me for so long. He spent an hour beating me. He hit me all over with his hand, belt and slipper in my bedroom. It happened again after a couple of weeks. I started to think, that's just what dads do.

His father's moods darkened. They moved out of Crompton Road to a new house in Birchfield Road, Perry Bar, just outside Birmingham. A few weeks later his mum and dad started rowing even more frequently. JaJa didn't know what the arguments were about but they were pretty ferocious. He stood, unseen, at the top of the stairs and listened as the voices of his parents got louder and more strained. He was too young to care what they were talking about. Instead he just focused on the terrible shouts that escalated into screaming and clattering. It was terrifying. He knew something bad was happening but didn't know what it was. One day, without warning, his mum took him and his brother and sisters back to Crompton Road. JaJa wanted to know why they moved but his mum wouldn't tell him.

The truth was that, for Sharon Kerr, life had never been the same since Delroy had gone to live in Ghana. For two years she hadn't heard a word from him. Not a word. No phone call. No letter. Nothing. She'd tried to find out from his friends what had happened but nobody would tell her. When he finally did come back she found it difficult to regain what they'd once had. That's why she'd decided to take the kids and move out. Sharon thought that after the temporary separation they might be able to rebuild a life together. Instead it got worse. Much worse.

Even though they weren't living together, Delroy kept turning up at the house ready for a fight. Sharon felt he was bullying her, implying that she wasn't a good mother.

His complaints came thick and fast.

'Why are you putting the kids in playschool? The staff will feed them the wrong food.'

He tried to make them wear African clothes that he'd brought back with him from Ghana.

'They should be wearing clothes that reflect where they are from.'

The rows exasperated Sharon Kerr and she hit back.

'It's cold. Why are they going to wear African clothes in this weather? You can't be telling them what clothes to wear.'

The kids had grown up and formed their own opinions while he was away. He couldn't take it. He couldn't take me backing the kids. I was brought up to be seen not heard and as far as I was concerned my kids were going to be heard. No one was going to come between me and my kids.

Delroy kept turning up at Crompton Road. Sharon tried to keep him out. But one day he just kicked the door down. This time JaJa wasn't in bed. He saw it all from the hallway. His father walked in and punched his mum. She came running out of the kitchen with a black eye. JaJa stood staring at her, tears forming in his eyes.

His mum tried to reassure him.

'Don't be crying. Please don't cry.'

Then she ran upstairs and locked herself in the bathroom.

When he hit my mum that's when it changed. When you are young your mum is everything in the world. And this guy hasn't been around very much and he comes back and punches her in the face, you think, what the hell?

JaJa was nine years old. He ran into the kitchen and got hold of a kitchen knife. When he came out his dad had already slammed the door and gone. Under his breath, though, he made a vow: Just wait till I'm older.

It never reached that point.

JaJa didn't know it, but his mum had already decided to act. She was going to take things into her own hands. She was finally sick of all the fighting, all the punch-ups. One evening, after months of abuse, the violence came to an abrupt conclusion.

Sharon had gone to play netball. It was the one activity that took her out of the home and gave her the chance to meet up with other women. She played on a team and had made some good friends. It was what she enjoyed doing. That evening, she'd taken the kids with her. She'd learned to drive some weeks before and she used to ferry herself and the kids to and from netball practice. She could tell that it had become an issue for Delroy. He resented the fact that Sharon was now independent and could drive herself around without his help. In spite of everything that had happened, JaJa's dad still liked to be the man of the house. He still turned up when he wanted and expected to find the family waiting. He expected everybody to ask his permission if they wanted something. Sharon had felt for some days that it was going to explode. So when Delroy turned up unexpectedly at the house after netball practice she almost knew what was going to happen.

'Where the fuck have you been?'

His face was pinched, his lips tight. He was a dense ball of festering rage.

'Tell me. Where the fuck were you?'

It was like a red rag to a bull. Sharon had grown up with a father who used to bully and intimidate both her and her mother. Her childhood had been miserable. Life had only got better when her parents had separated and her father had moved back to Jamaica. She had sworn then that she wouldn't let a man push her around again.

'You've got no fucking right to talk to me like that.'

She told him that she was allowed to do what she wanted and that they were separated and he couldn't just keep coming back into her life and ordering her around.

Delroy locked JaJa and the other kids upstairs in their bedrooms, and put their German shepherd dog Sam in the kitchen.

Sharon knew what was going to happen. Whenever Delroy was going to hit her he would lock the dog away so the dog wouldn't attack him.

She took a deep breath. *Here we go again.*

He smashed Sharon's brand new television that she had just bought from Currys. He turned over chairs and smashed a glass.

Then he punched her in the face.

Sharon fought back but he pushed her over, held her down on the ground and laid into her with his feet. She struggled and shouted and screamed at him. But he carried on kicking her as he held her down. It was during the kicking that Sharon made up her mind what she was going to do.

When the worst was over and he had gone upstairs she gingerly got to her feet, sat on the couch and called her friend.

'This can't go on. It's got to stop. I can't live like this. I'm gonna kill him.'

She had already planned it in her head. She was going to wait for him to fall asleep, then she would put a cushion over his face and stab him.

'I'm going to do it now. I have to do it.'

Her friend was silent for a while. Then she reminded Sharon that she had other responsibilities.

'If you kill him you'll be locked up and there won't be nobody to look after the kids.'

That sobered Sharon up. But she still knew that she would have to do something. If she didn't get out of there the next day she really would kill him. She meant it. She would kill him.

By that evening she had worked out her plan.

The next morning Sharon waited until she heard the door slam. It meant that Delroy had gone off to his job making bracelets and necklaces in Hockley, the jewellery quarter of Birmingham. She packed the kids off to school and went straight to social services.

'I need to get out of here.'

The woman at the counter could see how urgent it was. Sharon's face was black and blue.

'Where do you want to go?'

'I need to get far. We're going to London.'

Sharon's mother lived in north London. It was the only place where she knew someone she trusted and which was far enough away to be safe.

Social services rang round and found a women's refuge hostel in Tulse Hill near Brixton, south London.

Sharon thought that Brixton sounded good. She knew that Brixton had a large black community similar to Handsworth. It would help the kids fit in.

She went home, packed a suitcase and collected her passport and bank book. Then she walked, bent almost double with the pain from the kicking, to the bookies down the road where she worked. She explained to her boss what had happened. He was good about it. He gave her £400 in wages and wished her luck.

Then she went to the kids' school and spoke to the head teacher, Miss Dillon. The head teacher understood immediately and wrote her a letter to help get the kids into another school in London. Then she collected JaJa, Chantelle, Saffiya and Naja, took them home, sat them down and talked to them.

JaJa was shocked when his mum came out with it.

'I'm leaving. You can either stay here with dad or come with me.'

But he didn't hesitate.

'I'm coming with you.'

They were each allowed to pack their stuff into a small bag. They wanted to take their bikes and their other toys but Sharon explained that they couldn't take everything. Naja was the most upset. He wanted to take his Ninja robot that he had got the previous Christmas. It was too big to fit in his one bag. They left it behind with everything else. The TV and stereo and everything. They left it all behind. Before they closed the front door Sharon turned to JaJa.

'I know this is gonna be hard and you are going to hate me but I'll make it up to you.'

JaJa followed his mum out of the house, into a black taxi and from there to the coach station in New Street. His mother never told them why they were leaving. But he wasn't stupid. He knew why they'd left. He knew that they'd left there because his dad was hitting her. He knew that his dad was living with another woman.

'Where are we going?'

'We're going to London.'

On the coach JaJa tried to keep the strange feelings rising up in his stomach at bay by looking out at the changing landscape.

At Victoria coach station he watched his mum dial the telephone number of a women's hostel in south-west London.

JaJa knew that he wasn't going back to Birmingham. What he didn't know was that he would never see his father again.

The family was given temporary accommodation in a small room in the hostel. It was five metres by three metres. It was for the whole family; five of them with all their belongings. JaJa stood and looked out of the window.

I thought what the hell is this? We just come from a nice house, a big place, to somewhere new, somewhere I got no friends, and I thought I'm going to have to start all over again. I realized this was for real and we're not going back to Birmingham. In Birmingham I had mixed friends, Chinese, black, Asian friends. Now I had no friends and nothing and no one.

Sharon could see that her son was upset. She did what she could to comfort him.

'We're staying here now. Don't worry, we'll sort ourselves out. We'll find a house. We've just got to wait a little while. We've got to go through this rough stage for a bit. It's going to be hard at first, it's going to be horrible, but I'm going to make it right.'

JaJa felt like crying.

I went to the window by myself and I remember I looked out and tears started to go down my face. It was a little

*window and I thought, 'No way, where are we?' and the
tears kept coming. I remember it was a grey day and it had
just finished raining and it was dull outside. It just looked
strange. The whole atmosphere was just strange.*

His mum sat him down and talked to him again.

'Don't worry. It will get better. You'll start school soon and
meet some new friends.'

That calmed JaJa down a bit.

But he wasn't sure that he believed her. He just felt like crying
and crying. And he was amazed that his mum wasn't in tears too.

The truth was that even if Sharon Kerr had felt like crying there
was no time to fall apart. For the sake of the kids she had to show
that she wasn't scared. But she was scared. She was leaving a nice
house in Birmingham and heading into the unknown. She
knew it was going to affect the kids, uprooting them from their
schools and their friends. But she could see no other way out.
She now had a plan and she was determined to make it happen.
Her back was still hurting from the kicking that Delroy had giv-
en her in Birmingham. That spurred her on and reminded her
of why she had left.

As soon as she got settled into the Tulse Hill hostel she called
her mother who lived in Tottenham. Sharon hadn't brought
with her any of the kids' sheets or pillows or blankets and the
hostel didn't provide them so her mum told her to go to the TSB
bank in Tulse Hill and she would speak to her branch and get
the money sent over straightaway. Within hours of arriving,
Sharon was clutching £300 to spend on bedclothes. She deliber-
ately didn't tell her mum where she had taken the kids because

she knew that Delroy would try and find them and force them to go back to Birmingham.

The next day that's exactly what he tried to do.

Delroy turned up at Sharon's mum's house and banged on the door demanding to know where they were. When she refused to let him in, he kicked down the door. Sharon was glad that she hadn't told her mum where they were because she knew that she would try and get them to reconcile. That's the sort of person her mother was. She saw the good in everyone. She even saw the good in her violent and abusive boyfriend.

Talking to her mum the next day it was clear that Delroy was in shock. He couldn't and wouldn't believe that Sharon had just upped and left.

To this day he's still suffering from shock. To this day he has never got over the fact that we just walked out. We had to walk out. I had to protect me and my kids.

It was only a year or so later, when Sharon thought they were finally safe from being hassled by her former partner, that she told her mum where they were.

The hostel in Tulse Hill was small and dingy. But the next hostel they moved to was even worse. The room was even smaller and more cramped. There were six other families – Moroccan people and a white woman with mixed-race kids. Sharon was happier though. She began to talk to the other families and discovered that they'd all been through the same thing. JaJa too was happier. Gradually he got into the vibe and started playing with the other kids. On occasions he even managed to forget that they had come to a new place and that he would never go back to Birmingham.

street boys

By the time they were moved to temporary accommodation in Streatham Vale, JaJa even managed to feel as though he was blending in. He got put into a primary school in Brixton called Effra, and every morning he would take his brother and two sisters to school on the bus. Or rather buses. It took three buses and forty-five minutes to get to school. He hardly saw his mum. She had taken two jobs, one at McDonald's, the other a cleaning job. Most nights she wasn't back till very late, when he was already in bed. Sometimes he didn't see her for three days.

'Can you look after the others?'

'Yeah, don't worry, I can do it.'

He knew he was young but he believed he was sensible. It was a way of helping his mum. Sometimes he'd catch her in the morning and she'd ask how his day had been and he'd have to tell her that Naja had lost his bus pass or his lunch money, or that there had been some other mishap. She'd leave some money for him the next day and tell him to make sure that he looked after the younger ones. He grew up quickly. He could see how much his mum was doing for them and was determined to help her out. *Help out, help out.* That's the thought that went round and round his head.

One day he went up to his mum.

'Why do we live so far from school?'

Even from a young age he realized how much more difficult life was for them all if they had to travel an hour and a half to school and back every day.

'Don't worry; we'll get another flat closer by.'

His mum's promise, that they would soon be moving on, made life more bearable for JaJa.

Most of the time he and his brother and sisters just stayed

indoors. His mum's friend had driven her back to Birmingham and they'd returned loaded up with clothes, a television and a computer. They'd stolen into the Crompton Road house while his father had been out and taken what they could fit in the van. With a television and a computer JaJa and his brother and sisters felt happier about staying inside.

At the weekends and on summer evenings they would play with the two white kids, Luke and Perry, who lived next door, sometimes borrowing their bikes to ride up to the gypsy camp in the park. The Irish people there, intrigued by JaJa's strong Brummie accent, always had questions for him.

'You sound different. Where you from?'

He started getting nosier and nosier, venturing further and further afield. And then one day, Ross, a friend from the Effra School, asked him if he wanted to hang out at his house after school. That evening, JaJa asked his mum and she said it was OK.

A week later, when the bell rang at the end of the school day, Ross and JaJa walked out of the school gates, through the streets of Brixton to an estate just off the Brixton Road. JaJa was amazed. He had never been on an estate before. It was not the sort of thing he'd ever seen in Birmingham. But he immediately liked the area. There were raised pedestrian walkways connecting blocks of flats. There was a small park and a football pitch where other kids hung out. *This is OK here. This is a whole new area. It's totally different.* He liked the vibe. The atmosphere felt better, as though there was more going on. He felt he could fit in. He went back home and told his mum.

'We should try and live in Brixton. It's a good area for us.

Streatham Vale is too full of grannies. Let's go and live in Brixton. It's our kind of place.'

A month later his mum said they were going to look at a flat. They got off the bus and started walking along a road and into an estate. It took him some time to realize that the estate they had entered was the one where his friend Ross lived.

'This is where I come the other day.'

'Well, this is where we've got our new flat.'

They went to a large block of council flats called Marston House. They stood outside number 124.

'This is where we are going to live as soon as they've finished painting it.'

JaJa was so happy. There was music on the streets. Reggae and ragga music was blasting out from cars and open windows. Musicians called Shabba Ranks and Ninja Man rapped about sex and guns and violence. Kids were running around. It was a totally different atmosphere from the streets of Streatham Vale.

'What's this place called?'

'This is Angell Town.'

If Streatham Vale was a kid's nightmare, Angell Town, London SW9, was a kid's dream.

JaJa's mum hadn't picked Angell Town out. The truth was she didn't have a choice. The flat in Angell Town was the only one that came up and she had to take it. Life in Streatham Vale had become unbearable. The furniture there was from the 1970s, and the neighbours, particularly the old couple who lived next door, soon began to object to the presence of a single black mum with four noisy kids. They were always complaining that JaJa and his brother and sisters were making too much noise, that they played their music too loud, that they didn't belong there.

I don't blame them coz they bought their nice house in a residential area and the people next door rented it out to any Tom, Dick and Harry. That was us, a single mum with four rough kids from Handsworth in Birmingham and she had two nice little boys with blond hair. I don't blame them at all.

But soon the complaints turned into abuse. Sometimes Chantelle, JaJa's sister, would come home and tell Sharon that there were some kids who were spitting on her brother. When Sharon walked up to collect her kids from the park at the end of the road, curtains would twitch and people would throw things at her. One day there was a message written in black paint on her door.

'Go back home.'

She went straight to the housing department.

'Please move us. You got to move us. I don't care where you move me, just move me.'

It was one of the worst times of her life. Every week she went to the housing department at Lambeth Town Hall. There was always a queue of people waiting in line just to get a ticket. Sometimes the queue went right round the block. When she finally got a ticket she would find that she had number 105 and there were still fifty people in front of her. She would sit in a bare-walled waiting room with hard chairs and wait for hours for her number to be called. It was better when the kids finally got into school, but in the early days, while she was still in the hostel, she had to take them with her. After hours of hanging around in a boring waiting room they would get increasingly frustrated and Sharon would lose her temper.

'Elijah, stop that. Chantelle, stop crying.'

The four kids would start running around the waiting room, climbing on chairs and crawling around on the floor, making a racket. She would try and shut them up with food from packed lunches that she'd brought with her, but once the crisps and the Curly Wurly chocolate bars were gone the kids would go back to causing havoc. That's when the sly glances from other people in the waiting room would start and the muffled mutterings. The glances from other mothers in the waiting room would turn nasty and the huffing and puffing would become more exaggerated. Sharon knew what they were doing. They were looking at her and talking about her under their breath. They were saying she was a bad mum.

Finally her number would come up and it would be her turn at the counter.

'Have you got anything for me today?'

'No, sorry. Nothing today.'

What do you do? Do you go, 'I've been waiting here all day and that's all you can do? That's all you can say to me? I've waited six months and you still haven't got any accommodation you can put me in?' 'Course I said I'll take anything.

Sharon found the waiting and the hanging around for proper accommodation unbearable. So when a letter eventually arrived saying that somewhere had come up on an estate in Brixton she didn't think twice.

> *When that envelope from the housing people arrived saying that we could move to Angell Town, it was a proper relief. Finally, our own home. It was the best thing what happened to me.*

The housing people took her to a council block in Angell Town called Marston House. She was amazed. Like JaJa she'd never seen an estate before. When they opened the door of 124, Marston House, she was delighted. She had been in Streatham Vale for so long that she didn't mind that it looked like a dump. It had five bedrooms. *It's the biggest place I've ever seen. It's like a palace.*

When she finally got the keys, the kids ran in and each chose a room. The joy didn't last long. When Sharon opened the door later that day, a group of kids were standing there, looking at her threateningly.

> *It was proper scary when we first moved there but because we were desperate we didn't have no choice, so I didn't care. So I said to my kids I said, 'Remember where we come from, we're from Birmingham and no matter what happens, don't change the way we are.' And I don't think we never have. But that helped us because we got tested. From the same day we moved in we were tested. I was tested by them kids standing in front of the front door. It was like America. When I went out they were standing there and when I came back they were standing there.*

The flat had been a squat. A crack house. It was used by kids on the estate as a place where they could 'coch'; it was a place to smoke and drink, away from the prying eyes of their parents. The housing department had taken the flat back, given it a lick of paint and put in new, sturdy locks. But the kids still hung around. Sharon felt that she was marked. She got her kids together.

'Let's just stick together, nobody can't farce with us. Nobody can't mess with us coz if they do we are gonna fight.'

And she was ready to fight.

The next time she went out, she opened the door and spoke firmly to the kids hanging round outside.

'Can you move away from my door, please?'

It helped that she and her family were black but she was conscious that they weren't Londoners and that the other people living on the block were testing her to see how she would react.

When she came back she repeated her request.

'Can you move from my door, please?'

Slowly she began to ask the kids their names and even throw questions at them.

'Angell Town. Is it good? Is it nice round here? Where are the shops?'

It worked. They began to realize that they couldn't intimidate her. It wasn't long before Sharon, Elijah, Chantelle, Saffiya and Naja Kerr weren't the new kids on the block any more.

Chapter Three

Simon

Eight years old. That's when my life went downhill. From eight years old nobody looked after me. I just lived on the streets and made do by myself. There was no one except me and my friends.

Phat Si

Phat Si wasn't always Phat Si. That nickname came later. His first nickname was Fat Si. Fat because he was tubby, Si because he was born Simon Maitland from Stockwell, south London. His family lived on the west side of the Brixton Road, in a council house on the Stockwell Park Estate. He felt lucky that he'd been born into a happy and protective family. He was spoiled by his five sisters and loved by his mum and dad. He admired his dad. He was tall and big and good-looking and, unlike most of his friends' dads, he wore a suit and carried a briefcase like a proper businessman. Everyone loved his dad and wanted to hang out with him. But Si was most proud of his mum. She was beautiful. That's what he remembered most about her.

Beautiful, and, to his young eyes, elegant and statuesque.

He felt he was lucky to have such good parents. They threw birthday parties for him every year until he was eight years old. They were big parties, with cake and jelly and presents and all his friends and family around him. Life was good. Life was how it should be for little kids. That's when things began to change.

Eight years old.

One afternoon he came home from his school, St Helen's, which was just up the road from his house, and pushed open the back garden door which was always unlocked so that friends and neighbours could come and go without having to ring the doorbell. He expected to see the house full of fun and action. That's how it usually was.

This time it was different. He didn't hear the usual noise of kids running around, or his mum shouting at them to keep them quiet. He couldn't hear the clanging of pots in the kitchen or smell the waft of rice and beans being prepared for dinner. He knew then something was wrong. He just couldn't tell what. He pushed open the door, a sense of panic rising inside him.

I came home from school and there was no sign of my mum and my sisters. I had no idea. I was young. I didn't know what was going on. I pushed open the door and there was nothing in the house. There was no one. I was petrified. I was shocked, innit? One minute there was a family there and the next minute no one. It was a difficult stage for someone as young as me to go through. D'you get me?

Gripped by panic he ran through the house shouting for his mum. But there was nothing. There was no one. The TV was there and the sofa. But there were no records or books on the shelves. There were no clothes in his mum's wardrobe, no toys in his sisters' rooms. He didn't understand. Terrified by the empty house he ran up the road towards Brixton where his dad had a shop. It was a designer clothes store in Granville Arcade, just inside Brixton market. He ran breathlessly through the market bumping into disgruntled passers-by and found his dad slumped behind the till of the shop.

'Dad, there's no one in the house. Mum's not there.'

His dad gave him a sad, resigned look.

'I know. Your mum's gone.'

His dad already knew. He'd gone home earlier in the day and discovered it was empty. He told his son that he wouldn't be able to stay with him, that he didn't have the means to look after him and that Simon would have to live with his grandmother in John Ruskin Street in Camberwell. It was that simple. There was nothing else his father said. Maybe there was nothing else his father could say.

That evening his father led him by the hand to his grandma's house. And that's where Fat Si spent the first night the day his mum left.

My grandma explained my mum and dad got split up. She didn't explain why. She said my mum and sisters had gone to live in another country. It wasn't the same no more after that. I never understood why I'd been left behind. But I did understand that I was on my own.

From the moment that his mum left, Fat Si's life became more difficult. He found himself constantly angry and frustrated. At school he dropped his studies and did dumb stuff, like getting into fights and talking back to teachers. He was suspended. When he went back he fought some more. Then he was kicked out again. In the end he stopped going to that school altogether. His new school sent a letter to his father saying that his son's behaviour was so bad that from then on he was required to accompany his son to school and sit at the back of the class to keep him under control. His dad tried a couple of times and then gave up. Fat Si didn't mind. Instead of going to school he used to cross into the estate that was on the east side of Brixton Road. There were more kids there. Kids that he could hang out with, kids like Fat Chris, Michael Deans and the Cross brothers. There was more fun to be had there. The estate was called Angell Town.

Chapter Four

Nathan & Michael

It never really made no difference that my mum kicked my dad out because he was in and out all the time anyway. He never stayed every night. He had a room at my granddad's house so he never really lived with us. He used to come and drop off my school money but I never see him, coz he used to put the money through the letter box. He used to post my bus pass and school money. And once a month, like, he would get me a pair of trainers or something. He was there a little bit but he had so much kids elsewhere that I never really expected nothing from him, so …

Birdie

The Cross brothers lived in one of the twelve large council blocks that made up the Angell Town estate. Back then, before the boys took their street names of Inch and Biker, they were just Nathan and his younger brother Andrew. They lived with their devoutly Christian parents, older brother and three sisters in a small, four-bedroom flat in Pym House. Pym House, like the other council blocks, Marston House, Ireton House and Fairfax House, was a high-density council block, nearly 100 metres long and three storeys high with 130 small flats. It was at the heart of Angell Town. The estate had been designed and built in the 1970s as an attempt to regenerate the area. At the time it was thought of as 'visionary' architecture that would provide low-cost housing for 800 families and encourage community spirit. That's why the blocks in Angell Town were connected by a labyrinth of raised pedestrian walkways which the architects tried to invest with some romance by calling them 'pedways'. But already by the late 1980s the estate was sinking into decay and instead of being called Angell Town was referred to as 'Hell's Gate'. Residents had begun to complain that the network of open garages underneath the council blocks attracted rats and cockroaches and was a hang-out for drug pushers, flashers and rapists. They complained that the 'pedways' provided an escape route for muggers and house burglars. Even the concrete football pitch at the centre of the estate came in for criticism. Kids used to come back with grazed knees from falling on the hard, gritty surface, and mothers complained that the high wall surrounding the pitch meant that they couldn't keep an eye on what their kids were doing. Not that kids like the Cross brothers noticed. Even though their mother kept them on a tight rein, Nathan and Andrew Cross still enjoyed running around the estate, hiding beneath the pillars of the 'pedways' and hanging out with Fat Chris, Fat Si and Michael Deans on the estate's solitary green space. It was a small, run-down park littered with broken glass and beer cans. For the Cross brothers, though, it was a place of pure romance, a gateway to another world where they could watch the older boys smoke dope and drink beer. Along with Fat Si and Michael Deans, they would spend hours on the broken, graffiti-scarred bench dreaming that one day they too would be flirting with the girls and showing off their latest pair of American trainers.

One summer, Nathan, the older of the Cross brothers, noticed a new kid hanging out in the Angell Town park. It was a kid with a strange accent. Nathan had heard strange accents before. He had family that came from Moss Side in Manchester but this kid had a different accent. A strong accent. He went up to the new boy.

'Where you from?'

'Birmingham.'

'What's your name?'

'Elijah.'

Nathan wanted to hear him carry on talking because the accent was so funny. Soon both the Cross brothers were asking him questions and getting him to talk more so that they could hear his accent. They found out he had a younger brother called Naja and that he had just moved into Marston House, the next block along the road from Pym House.

Nathan found himself being slightly surprised when, a week later, they all met up again and the boy's accent was as strong as it had always been.

* * *

'Who are those Sheffield kids?'

That was Michael Deans's first question to the Cross brothers when he saw the new kids in the park. He'd been to Barbados to visit relatives with his mum and hadn't been there during JaJa's first week in Angell Town.

'That's Elijah and Naja. And they are not from Sheffield. They are from Birmingham.'

That evening, Michael Deans discovered that Elijah and Naja had moved into Marston House next door to the flat he lived in with his parents, two sisters and little brother.

Michael Deans, who would later go by the street name of Birdie, had known the Cross brothers for as long as he could remember. Michael's father and Nathan's father used to 'roll' or hang out together. Because the kids were the same age they used to hang out together too. They were different characters, though. Michael was quiet and thoughtful. The Cross brothers were wilder, more energetic. Michael Deans' first shock in life was when his mother kicked his dad out. She didn't say anything. She just left black bin bags with his belongings outside the front door. He'd been sleeping around and rarely came home at night. Michael was eight years old. But after the initial shock though, he didn't really notice his dad's absence.

My dad's got a lot of kids all over. He never hid that we had brothers and sisters all over the place ... and I had enough of that crap. There were never arguments in front of us, so it didn't affect me much.

His dad had been born in Jamaica and was in the music business. He was a drummer who used to play old reggae stuff. His mum was from Barbados and they'd met and started their relationship in Balham, a few miles west of Angell Town. The only time Michael saw his dad was about once a month when he used to drop off the school money. After a time, though, he just posted it through the letter box. It was his mum who gave them all her energy. She made sure that they sat at table and said prayers before dinner like a proper family.

Nathan Cross and Michael Deans were pleased with their new friend, Elijah. They were pleased that they had someone else to muck around with on the estate. They were especially pleased because a few weeks earlier Fat Si had gone away. It was a shock. Fat Si had been with them on the Angell Town estate for as long as they could remember, often spending the night at Fat Chris's in Pym House so that he wouldn't have to go and live with his grandmother in Camberwell. But now Fat Si had gone. And nobody knew when, or if, he'd be back.

And that's how it started. Four little boys, Elijah, Simon, Nathan and Michael, who would take the street names of JaJa, Phat Si, Inch and Birdie. Soon they would be joined by three others, Bloods, Ribz and Tempman. Seven kids who would grow up together in Angell Town and become the core of the most notorious gang in south London.

Chapter Five

Fat Si in 'the Jungle'

That's how advanced I was as a little boy. I was forced to fend for myself. Ever since I was eight years old I've lived on the streets and had to look after myself.

Phat Si

Fat Si's father hadn't been able to cope with his son. Fat Si's wild behaviour and constant truancy got too much for him. He paid for Fat Si to get on a plane and go and live with his mother. She was in Toronto, Canada. Fat Si was delighted to be going. He'd heard good stories about Canada. His grandmother had told him that his mum had relatives there and that's why she'd moved. It still bothered him that his mum hadn't taken him with her but he wanted to see her and his sisters again so badly that he pushed it from his mind. He wanted to get out of England. He'd got frustrated living with his grandmother in her small house in Camberwell. *What sort of life is that for a young kid, living with an old woman?* He'd ended up spending most days kicking around Angell Town and most nights kipping with friends who lived on the estate.

He got himself to Heathrow and flew alone from Heathrow to Toronto. Fat Si was 11 years old. His trip started to go wrong from the moment he landed.

I'd wanted to be with my mum and sisters but forgot that my dad wouldn't be there. My mum wasn't at the airport to meet me. Just my grandma and my sister. And the house was worse than in England. My mother had another little girl with a different dad and it was chaotic. There were eight of us in a three-storey house. But the front room was mum's bedroom. There was three feet of snow and that. There was rats and moths. The house wasn't fit for no one to live in it. It was not a good environment to raise kids in. I had to go to school in my sister's cast-off clothes and wear her sweaters and jeans and trainers. It was embarrassing, weren't it?

The house was in an area near the Jane and Finch corridor in a district of Toronto called 'the Jungle', named after a West Kingston neighbourhood back in Jamaica. There were jerk chicken and jerk fish shops and Jamaican grocery stores in the surrounding streets. Reggae blasted out from boom boxes all day and all night long. But Fat Si wasn't happy. Even though his mum had family in Toronto, there was never enough money to go round. Fat Si felt that his maternal grandmother had misled them. She had persuaded Fat Si's mum to leave England for a rich, new life in Canada. Instead they were living in a damp, cold house that was falling down with hardly enough money for basic food. And Fat Si didn't react well to his new surroundings.

*They were difficult times. Instead of helping, I added to the
problem. I got into bad company straightaway. I was going
to the community centre and smoking weed and getting
drunk. The family from my mum's side were there. I got on
all right with them. But I spent my time stealing and
causing havoc.*

After a few months he got into so much trouble that no one
minded when he said that he wanted to go back to England. He
missed his dad. He made a reverse charge call and asked for a
ticket back home. He didn't know how his dad got hold of the
money but it wasn't long before he was booked on a ticket back
to London. He didn't ask his mum whether he could go. Ever
since he was eight years old he didn't ask anybody anything. He
just did everything himself.

When he got to the airport in Toronto he was lucky to leave
without problems. He'd already outstayed his six-month tourist
visa. He'd been in Canada illegally. He hadn't known it but his
mother had been given refugee status and had applied for resi-
dency for herself and her six daughters. But not for Fat Si, her
only son. It was summer 1990, and Fat Si was on a plane back to
London, and Angell Town.

Chapter Six

Guns and Yardies

Maybe he felt incarcerated. Maybe that's what got him into trouble in the first place. Elijah was always that child who could never sit still. He never got enough freedom. Putting us on that estate made life worse. Maybe that's where it went wrong. Because he stayed on the estate, he used the resources on the estate. That was all he knew and so that's all he took.

Sharon Kerr

The nocturnal activities outside Marston House fascinated JaJa. From the age of 11 he stood on tiptoes looking out of the kitchen window at the procession of outsiders coming into Angell Town. He had a view over the whole estate. He watched them wander towards the open stairwell at Marston House and engage in some sort of shady business with the older boys who were gathered down below. Evening after evening he would stand there and watch them until he began to figure out the routine.

I see guys out there from my window and I used to see things going down. I got to see street life properly. There is a block

*of flats over there and another one over there and I see the
drug addicts and I see them walk up to guys over there
smoking weed. I'm seeing loads of transactions and loads of
different things. I watch closer, day after day, and I start
realizing their routine. That's the drug dealer. He's selling
drugs to those guys and that guy sells weed to those people
there. There are some girls over there but I don't know what
they are doing but there are a set of thieves over there and
burglars over there.*

He worked out that as soon as it got dark someone would bring
plastic bags full of weed into the estate. Then one of the others
would go out into the streets of Brixton and let the punters know
that the drugs were available. He learned that punters were called
'cats' and that they would sometimes hand over large amounts of
money in return for the bags of weed. He learned to distinguish
between the different groups that hung around in the streets
below. The ones in the open stairwell underneath Marston House
sold weed to one group of 'cats'. Another group of older boys in
the streets by Pym House were selling blocks of something called
'Brown' to a different group of 'cats'. He learned to distinguish
between the British-born black boys who used to hang around
the block and who called themselves 'the 28s' and the older boys
who were born in Jamaica and who everyone called 'Yardie Men'.

It wasn't long before the older boys started to recognize
JaJa too.

*These boys come up to me and were saying where are you
from, what accent is that. We talked and they introduced me
to others on the estate. I saw the big boys and the block*

where the crack house was. There was always people hanging outside. The crack addicts and drug dealers were always hanging around. That's how I got to know the big boys. People knew me because of my accent. They called me 'Birmingham'. The big boys would say, 'There's little Birmingham. Come Birmingham, come.' That's how I got to hang around with the big boys.

His mum started a night job which meant that as the summer went on he went to bed even later and could stand at the window, undisturbed, observing the goings on in Angell Town till late at night.

As the moon came out he noticed that a new breed of nightlife would take over the streets. Girls would gather and stroll around in the open areas of the estate and either go into someone's house or get into a passing car. Another group of Yardies would gather and talk about stolen TVs and snatched handbags. They talked about 'tiefing tings' or stealing things.

A whole new set of wild people come out. They are on the landing and talking and they can't see me and I can hear everything they are saying so I would hear stuff about shootings and robberies and tiefing car stereos. I heard everything.

'You bin hearing about dat big somebody dat got shot in Stockwell?'

'Dat other big man him tief nuttin' but ganja.'

'You wahn se de money he tief?'

'Dat man he got shot dead. He da one with da stolen car.'

One evening he couldn't quite hear what the group of men were saying so he leaned further out of the window. One of the older boys looked up and saw him.

'Hey, Birmingham. What ya doin'? You should be in de bed. I'll tell you mama.'

JaJa looked down and, because he was nosy, threw back a question of his own.

'What's that in your hand?'

The older boy looked up at him and held up a car stereo and a small bit of white metal. JaJa didn't know it at the time but it was a spark plug.

'What's that?'

'You throw dis at de car window and de window i' shatters. Den you tief da pull out.'

The whole atmosphere made its mark on JaJa.

They had lots of gear on at the time, and they had flashy stuff, like new pairs of jeans and flashy gear and Nikes. I'm really impressed coz I've only got mummy clothes. I thought 'OK' and this is going on for a while and they are showing me stuff like bags of weed and that.

There was a constant aromatic smell on the landing and in the stairwells. He recognized it because his dad used to smoke. Now he realized that the smell came from the bags of small leaves that the older boys carried around in plastic bags. He wanted to know more.

'What's that?'

'See dis. Dis is a £10 bag of ganja. And dis is a £20 one.'

It carried on like that every night. Each time they gave him more information.

After a while I knew more and more about these things and the lifestyle is kicking in and they are seeing that I don't really know for real and that I'm fascinated and I'm a young guy trying to grow up and they see I am not scared to ask.

One evening at about 9.30 one of the Yardies shouted up to him. His mum was still out working.

'Hey, Birmingham. Me friend has to go over to dat house over there and get him TV and computer, so if you see any big somebody or policemen, let me know because I need to talk to dem.'

JaJa was impressed by his newly acquired responsibility.

So I'm thinking I'm doing something good. The big boy wants me to do something for him. I'm involved. So I'm there like a prat at the window and I see him climbing up to the window. He does something with a screwdriver, does something to the window and I hear a snap and he climbs into the window and he is inside for about half an hour and I was like, what's he doing? Then he comes out of the front door with a black bag and he comes back over the bridge from the landing and walks down to my window and calls up at me.

'Tank you, man. Did you see big somebody?'
'No. I didn't. Do you want me to call them? The police?'
'No, safe little man. It's OK. Don't do that.'
The older boy then threw JaJa a Game Boy.

It was the latest version.

'Yo, Birmingham. Keep it. Tell you mama you found it on dat landing. Don't tell her I gave it you.'

JaJa ran inside with it. He was delighted but decided to hide it under his bed. He never told his mum about it.

A few days later, another of the older boys was passing as JaJa played in the streets below. He held out a .45 revolver, real rusty and big.

'Hey, Birmingham. Take. Look after dis for me.'

JaJa was pleased. He took it as a sign that the older boy was respecting him. He didn't ask what the revolver was for. He buried it in the balcony garden outside his flat and when his mum wasn't around showed it to his friends. For three months he looked after that revolver. It gave him 'ratings' among the other kids on the block. It gave him respect. Then one day the older boy came and took it away. JaJa was 13 years old.

It was summer when Fat Si arrived at Heathrow on a British Airways flight from Toronto. His dad met him at the airport. They were pleased to see each other. They went back to his dad's flat. His dad told him that he wouldn't be able to stay with him because he had a new girlfriend. He said he'd have to go and live with his grandmother in Camberwell again. His dad gave him some money and Fat Si went straight off and bought a draw of weed. Then he headed off to Angell Town to find Fat Chris and the Cross brothers. The Cross brothers were so happy to see him that Andrew, the younger brother, ran up to him and hugged him.

I came straight round to the estate with my weed. They

*were all there. There was also a new guy there. His name
was Elijah, innit? He's from Birmingham. The day I come
back we ended up as pals. I don't know how that happened.
He brought me to his house, the same night I slept on the
couch in his house. His mum looked after me and I stayed
with him for about three weeks as soon as I got off that
plane. I should have been to my gran's house. Everyone was
looking for me but ever since then it's been me, Elijah and
Inch. We've been through a lot, d'you get me?*

Like JaJa, Nathan Cross was also fascinated by the goings on
around the Angell Town estate. But he didn't have the freedom
that JaJa had. His family was strictly Christian and he wasn't
allowed to hang out on the estate. He was expected to be back in
his bed in the family flat in Pym House by nightfall. If he wanted to go out he had to sneak past his parents' bedroom and open
the front door carefully. But he didn't do it often. He just carried on going to church, doing well with school and keeping up
his innocent persona. The only time he was allowed out was
when there was an official event at the Angell Town clubhouse
just down the road from Marston House.

The clubhouse was run by Fat Wayne's mum, a woman
called Dora Boatemah. Dora had got sick of the crime on the
estate. Her neighbours had complained of muggings, cars
being broken into, drug dealers squabbling into the early hours
of the morning. She was putting pressure on Lambeth Council to regenerate parts of the estate. That's why she started a
letter-writing campaign to the media and government figures.
She'd even been to the Houses of Parliament where she had
berated the then Minister for the Environment, Nicholas

Ridley, for coming up with grandiose but impractical regeneration schemes which didn't benefit the residents of estates like Angell Town.

'You've got all these proposals and it's OK for you to come up with them but you don't live down here and you don't know what it's like. You come down and live down here then you can see what goes on. The boilers are all broken in the winter and they come back on in the summer. Nothing works properly. Come and see for yourself.'

The Minister declined her invitation but her public berating of him got her respect and attention.

It started slowly at first with schemes to help mothers out by laying on crèches and coach trips to Margate during the school holidays. Most of the kids on the estate had never been to the seaside before. Then her letter-writing campaign began to get real attention.

Throughout the 1980s headlines in the local newspapers screamed: 'New Estate is Near Disaster', 'Misery of Life on Local Council Estate' and 'Report Demands a Quick Solution'.

Public and government opinion was firmly on her side. A decade earlier, riots in the centre of Brixton had led to a government enquiry by Lord Scarman that had criticized the police and the local authorities for discriminating against Brixton's black residents. Dora Boatemah now had the support of the council and the Department of the Environment. Soon she had pulled in a £3 million grant for a pilot scheme to convert the dingy garages underneath the Angell Town council blocks into workshops. It started with a launderette, a crèche and a place for senior citizens to meet and have a cup of tea. But what the younger kids appreciated most was that one of the burnt-out and derelict garages in the heart of Angell Town had been turned into a brand new clubhouse.

In the evenings, Nathan Cross, Elijah and the other young kids would gather outside the clubhouse and glare enviously at the older boys from the estate who were inside at the club's weekly dancing competition, showing off their Jamaican dancehall moves and fancy footwork routines. The older boys were known as 'the 28s' and the younger kids looked up to them with respect. They were cool, dressed in snazzy clothes and used street names with each other. To Nathan and Andrew Cross the use of street names made the 28s impossibly glamorous. Even though they were only 11 years old, the Cross Brothers wanted some of that glamour for themselves.

Gradually they took up their own street names like the older boys. Nathan became Inch because he was so short. His brother Andrew became Biker because he liked bikes. The fashion spread. Michael Deans became Birdie because, on the football field, he was quick on his feet. Errol Cole became Skippy because he was always disappearing. Michael Payne became Sykes, taking the same street name as one of the older boys in the 28s who looked just like him. There were others: Ham, Harvey, Fat Chris, Fat Wayne and Blacker. Soon their birth names were almost forgotten, banished to the confines of the classrooms. Around the council blocks of Angell Town it was street names that ruled, giving the young boys a status and an intimacy which subtly and secretly began to bind them together. The foundations were being laid for the day when they would replace the 28s as the most influential gang on the streets.

Chapter Seven

The 28s

*In those days it was about peace and unity. Life on the estate
was chilled. It wasn't like it is today with all the guns and
gangs and violence.*

Pod

One of the older boys who used to be at the Angell Town
clubhouse showing off his dance moves was Roger
Samuels. He went by the street name of 'Pod'. A woman from
Liverpool who lived on the estate had made the mistake of calling him 'podgy' in front of his friends. From then on, everyone
called him 'Pod'. He and the others in the 28s used to gather at
the clubhouse to meet up with girls before heading off to their
'coch'. That's what they called the empty and half-derelict flats
in the council blocks where they could smoke, drink alcohol,
party and sleep with their girlfriends without being disturbed
by parents or annoying neighbours. As soon as they got wind
that one of the council flats had emptied, they would kick the
door down and turn it into their own place where they could

hang out. It was the best place to have sex. Few parents on the estate would allow their sons' girlfriends into the family home, let alone into their sons' bedrooms.

That's how Pod lived. Chilling in the 'coch', dancing at the clubhouse and meeting up in the stairwell of Marston House with the other 28s like Duffers, Sykes, Keith Weed, Wesley, Maddix, Gummy, Hustler and Perry, to plan what they would get up to that evening.

'Let's go to a funfair.'

'Yeah we could do some robbing up there.'

'And find some girls.'

The talk was all about what they planned to do next, where they could go to have some fun, what they could rob without getting caught.

They were careful, though, about where they went to commit their crimes. They stayed clear of robbing anyone on the estate. In fact, often one of the neighbours would lean out of one of the balcony windows and shout down to them.

'We're going out for the rest of the evening. Will you keep an eye on the flat for me?'

Even when one of the neighbours went back to Jamaica for the holidays they would be happy to watch out for the flat.

They took pride in keeping their estate free of outsiders.

If the gang discovered that one of the flats had been burgled on their watch it would send a surge of adrenaline through them. Over the following days they would be doubly vigilant and one of them would always be on the lookout for any strangers hanging around. If someone came into Angell Town who they thought might be responsible for the burglary they would give them a good kicking. No one came into Angell Town without the permission of the 28s.

There was nothing mysterious about the origin of their name. The gang was made up of a core group of kids who'd all gone to the Tulse Hill School in Brixton. 'The 28s' wasn't an arcane reference to American gangsta culture, or to a London postcode or the lyrics of some Jamaican reggae song. Pod knew where it came from because he was there at the beginning.

We were called 'the 28s' because there were about twenty-eight of us.

Pod had grown up just as Angell Town was going through a slow transformation. In the late 1970s and early 1980s, life in Angell Town had been chilled, almost laid back. Social life on the estate had been built around the Jamaican-style 'sound systems' which were strung up in back gardens and around the Angell Town football pitch. During the weekend the smell of barbecued chicken and marijuana wafted through the council blocks to the soundtrack of chilled reggae music reverberating from huge boom boxes.

The estate attracted Jamaican DJs from all over London. They would come to Angell Town to play their own version of popular Jamaican sounds like Coxone or Saxon or Dread Diamonds.

If Pod was lucky, his father, who was the stern but respected local Christian preacher, would allow him to join the street parties and meet up with the other kids in the area. They ran from one sound system to another, fascinated by the dreadlocked DJs in their red, gold, black and green Rasta berets and by the swaggering Yardies dressed in long black coats and baseball caps and dripping with jewellery. Sometimes, though, his father would have the hump and wouldn't let him out. Then he would be forced to observe the excitement from the balcony of Pym House.

There were never fights or arguments. It was a time of peace and unity. The police wouldn't even need to come round because it was so chilled. They left the community alone and the community left the police alone.

It was rare that Pod got into any trouble. His father was a respected man in the community and set a good example. The only time Pod managed to get away from his father's steely gaze was during those Sundays when he sneaked out of church. That's when he would meet up with the other kids at the foot of Pym House. But as soon as they heard the church van bringing his father back home, they would 'chip', or run away. His father was so ferocious that no one wanted to hang around when he came back.

'Get away from my doorway. Leave this area.'

That's what he would say to any of the kids who inadvertently hung around the landing of Pym House. He was more than just the local pastor. He was a big man with a big temper and a big presence. Everyone did as he said.

At 13, Pod was allowed further afield. He went to break-dancing competitions at Brixton Recreation Centre, and body-popped with other kids from estates in Peckham and Clapham to see who was the best break-dancer. He played in the local Metropolitan Police five-a-side football competition organized by a community police officer whose name was Sergeant Hill. Pod's team, Angell Town's Mini Strikers, used to play other teams from all over south London. The matches, like the break-dancing competitions, created a rivalry with kids from other estates round south London. But the rivalry was always friendly.

That was lift-off for me. I was still quite podgy, but I was snappy with a ball at my feet. Those days crime wasn't high and most guys in my age group weren't doing anything bad. Even though we had competitions with other estates, it was all peaceful.

But that's when life on the estate started to change. That's when the 28s came into conflict with the Untouchables.

The Untouchables weren't strictly a local gang. While the 28s were made up of kids who lived in Brixton, the Untouchables had their roots 'northside', in north London. Through family ties and connections formed in prison, the gang's reputation had spread throughout south London until there were as many as sixty young guys who professed allegiance to the Untouchables living in Brixton. Some of the Untouchables had even turned one of the empty flats in Angell Town into their own 'coch' where they lived and partied. In the early days the 28s didn't mind because some of them were related by blood to the Untouchables.

But as the 1990s began, clashes between the gangs became pointed.

Pod first noticed it during the 'All Dayers' held at the Bogle Factory in Somerleyton, just across the road from Angell Town. That's when the so-called 'clash of sounds' was held. Different sound systems from all over London would meet up in an old factory and try to outdo each other with their music. The events would start at midday and go on until midnight. Pod and his crew would turn up with his sound system called 'King Agony'. The idea was that he would compete with rival sound systems from neighbouring estates in Kennington or Clapham or Peckham with names like 'Goldrush' or 'Silver Star'. Each sound system would have ten minutes to play their own unique type of music, often competing for 'Specials' or 'Dubplates'. That meant receiving a mention or praise during the set of one of the local rival sound systems, or even better from one of the bigger, more recognized sound systems like 'Nasty Love' or 'King Tubbies'. Getting a 'Special' or mention from a rival, especially a bigger rival, was a real accolade. But that's when the trouble would start. The rivalries were fierce, and sometimes, if a sound system felt slighted, the different crews would turn on each other. And because each sound system had its roots in different areas of London, the fighting would end up as clashes between different council estates.

If during one of the weekend All Dayers the clashes had been particularly nasty, the rivalries would often spill over into the working week, distilling down into rivalries between different gangs. And that's when the 28s and Untouchables would clash.

To start with it wasn't much more than chasing the Untouchables out of the estate or tracking some of their members down and stealing stuff from them. Bottles and stones were thrown. Sometimes there would be fist fights.

Looking back, though, it was still innocent. There were no knives or nothing. No guns. It was quite often about staring up each other.

'Staring up each other' – that's what Pod would do on a Saturday evening if there was nothing else going on. It meant that they would just stare at each other, looking for a fight. Sometimes it was with guys from the Untouchables, or strangers who'd walked uninvited into the estate. Sometimes the 28s used to fight amongst themselves. Pod would just stare at someone until a punch was thrown in anger. Then they'd end up brawling on the ground. It was rare that anyone took on Hustler, though. He was one of the main men in the 28s. The others looked up to him because he had a reputation as an effective and fearsome fighter. Most people tended to leave him alone.

It was on evenings like this, as the 28s gathered to fight or to chat about girls and robbing, that Pod became aware that some of the little kids on the estate had begun to hang around. Kids like Elijah Kerr, the Cross brothers, Michael Deans, Fat Chris and Michael Payne.

He'd watched most of them grow up. He knew Elijah Kerr, or JaJa as he was called, from the day he'd arrived from Birmingham as a little kid with a strange accent who'd looked lost on an estate like Angell Town. He'd known Nathan Cross, or Inch as he was called on the streets, from church and from Angell Town's steel band where he'd been the quiet little guy who played the drum and performed in front of Princess Diana and the Queen.

He'd watched them all grow up and change, becoming more confident, bolder, cheekier.

JaJa was the one who impressed him most. The kid always stuck up for himself, even when some of the older kids tried to bully him because of his thick Brummie accent. He always seemed to be one step ahead of the game.

Increasingly they'd begun to hang around the 28s, asking for money or just pestering them for no reason.

Now and then Pod would feel protective and dip into his pocket and pull out a handful of loose change which he would give to one of the kids. Then he would send them on their way with a kick up the backside.

'Stop bothering us. Here's some money. Now go and buy me some jerk chicken and a coke.'

Sometimes they refused.

'Why do we have to?'

'Coz we're older.'

'That don't make no difference.'

'Do what I say or I'll come after you.'

Sometimes the kids would hide for a week because they thought that Pod or one of the others really was after them.

The kid who Pod had most trouble with was the one everyone called Fat Si. Pod could see that the kid lived on the edge and had a short fuse. Pod enjoyed taunting him, seeing how far he could push him before getting a reaction. It was easy because Fat Si was always hanging around Pym House with Inch and JaJa. Whenever Pod saw Fat Si he would give him a kick in the leg.

Then one day Fat Si was waiting for him.

It happened on the landing of Pym House. Pod, as usual, was teasing Fat Si. He gave him a kick up the backside to taunt him. This time Fat Si whipped out a knife and stabbed Pod in the leg.

Pod screamed in shock and surprise.

'What the fuck did you do that for? I'm gonna knock you down.'

Fat Si didn't back down. He tensed up, ready to fight.

'I'm gonna get you for this.'

But Pod's leg was bleeding so badly that he hurried off to hospital to have it stitched up.

Pod left Fat Si alone after that. He'd found Fat Si's limit and didn't want to test him again.

He understood it, though. The whole estate knew that Fat Si's mum had run away to another country and left him to fend for himself.

He didn't have no motherly love. Lucky his dad always knew where he was. Even though his dad wasn't always around he always knew where Si was. They were always tight.

But still, Pod wondered, *if Fat Si is prepared to pick up a knife at the age of 11, what's he gonna do at 16?*

It wasn't long before Pod and the others in the 28s realized that the little kids they'd seen growing up on the estate had got older, bigger and more impertinent. Now they were roaming around the council blocks in their own group. That's when people on the estate began to make a joke of it.

'There go the Younger 28s.'

Chapter Eight

The Younger 28s

I saw what they were doing. But I wasn't stupid.
I thought, I could do this myself and keep the money.

JaJa

JaJa followed the lives of the 28s with fascination. At night, as Wesley, Pod and Duffers gathered with the other 28s beneath his window at Marston House, he would hang on their every word as they lit up joints and chatted about girls and robbing. They were famous. Famous because they were older and cool and famous because they had money. JaJa was now getting into his second year of school and he started realizing all the things that money could get him.

One day after school he went up to one of the 28s.

'Hey man, how do I get hold of my own money?'

'Hey, Birmingham. I tell you what. Come out with us tonight and watch. Just watch.'

That evening he asked his mum if he could go out with friends. He didn't have a curfew so she just told him to be careful and not come back too late. Some of the older boys gave him some weed. He spluttered on his first draw but then started getting the hang of it. Then he followed the older 28s boys to a small car around the corner from the estate. They grabbed hold of the top of the passenger door and bent it back.

Because I was so little I could squeeze my hand in and open the locks. That's what we used to do. And we'd hit the car stereos which we sold for 15 or 20 quid to an Italian guy called George. And when you are young, that's a lot of money. I used to get six stereos a night and I'd get 25 quid and I'm loving it 'cos we're doing this every two days. I'm getting change in my pockets. I got into the street life and that, buying weed and chilling with girls my age. I'd go into Brixton and meet more 28s and got to know more people and started to do house burglaries.

JaJa found the burglaries scary at first, but the older boys reassured him.

'No, don't worry, come. Just watch this one. Watch and see how we do it.'

It wasn't long before they got him to help them. They walked past a house with no lights on and would send JaJa to knock on the front door.

'Just go up, and if someone answers the door, ask for Stuart.'

JaJa did what he was told. He knocked on the door of a big house in Brixton. The porch light went on and the door opened.

'Is Stuart there?'

'No, mate. Stuart doesn't live here.'

'Oh, sorry. Wrong house.'

Then they would move on to the next house. This time it might be empty. JaJa would stay outside while the others would jimmy open a window and they would come out with everything they could lay their hands on. They'd store it all in a cupboard in someone's flat, then take it round to George's the next day. George introduced them to people who would buy the TVs and music equipment. JaJa got a cut each time, sometimes as much as £70. He now had money for weed and trainers.

That's when a new thought struck him.

I thought, this was good. But I also thought I could do this by myself. I don't really need those guys. I could do this with my friends and get more money for me. I could get more than £70.

In Angell Town, a school friend of JaJa's, a white boy named Mark, had noticed JaJa's new trainers.

'How come you always got all this new gear?'

JaJa told him about the burglaries he was doing. After school one day the same kid came back to him and introduced him to some older white guys.

'We're doing some bigger houses, mansions and that sort of thing in Clapham and posh areas. Come and join us. Don't stick around these poor areas.'

JaJa went along with them and got a whole new perspective on burglary. They would force open a window and get inside. These were bigger houses. Sometimes the alarm would go off and they would all have to leg it. But if they got in, they usually hit the jackpot.

*I'd go round the house and pick up TVs and stereo
equipment and the white guys would be saying, 'No, leave
all that. That's rubbish. Come, come.' They would open
little containers and drawers and pull out passports and
jewellery. And I would say, 'What you doin'? That's not
money.' They told me about Cartier and at one of the
burglaries they found a Cartier watch and one of them said
that costs more than everything else in the flat. I was upset
because I thought it was a waste of time but when we came
back out they gave me £360. And then I thought, this was it;
these guys know what they're doing.*

Then one of the older white men went to jail. Then Mark was
arrested. So JaJa stayed away from them. Instead he went back
to Angell Town and with Nicky and Skippy and some of the
other guys they started doing their own burglaries. Soon there
was a buzz on the streets about the Younger 28s. What started as
a group of kids aping what the older boys did had turned into a
fully-fledged, tight-knit gang.

The Younger 28s weren't that careful, though. They didn't
wear gloves. One day, when JaJa was getting ready for school
there was a knock on the door and footsteps in the hallway.
Three white men dressed in badly fitting grey suits came in.

'Are you Elijah Kerr?'

JaJa nodded.

'You are arrested on suspicion of burglary.'

Someone had recognized JaJa's jacket and reported him.
They now wanted to take a set of his fingerprints. He wasn't
scared, but his mum was furious. She started cussing him. JaJa

took no notice of her complaints. It was the same old mummy stuff.

'You'll turn out just like your dad.'

JaJa knew, though, that she must have known what he was doing with his life. How else did she think he managed to afford so many pairs of new trainers?

But what could she do? She tried to slap him and beat him but he was a man now and could do his own thing.

They took him to Brixton police station. His fingerprints matched. The CID cops also discovered that his prints matched those found at ten other crime scenes.

JaJa didn't mind. He was too young to go to prison. He barely cared when they gave him probation and three years community service.

For JaJa it was a waste of time. He'd turn up to see the probation officer.

'Is everything OK?'

'Yes.'

'OK, see you next week.'

Sometimes he would get to go karting but he didn't really see the point of it all. It didn't stop him offending.

Then at school he pushed a teacher. He was prancing around with a ticket that he had bought for a music event. He was boasting to his friends that he had money and could afford to go out at night. The teacher came over and ripped it away.

'You can't have that in here.'

The whole class laughed. JaJa felt his body taken over by a fury of embarrassment. He couldn't take it. He stood up and pushed the teacher. JaJa couldn't quite believe it when she toppled over and fell to the floor.

I thought my mum was going to go sick on me and I thought I'm really going to get it. The next day, a letter came saying what happened. And she started cussin' me and whacked me with a belt. She really hit me and as she was hitting me I was thinking, what are you doing that for? And I started smiling. I started smiling because I realized I was too big for beatings. She was thumping me and I was holding her hands. I was old now and I knew she couldn't beat me no more. When you are a kid you think, 'You've got to look after me,' that's what she is there for. That's her job. She's a mum. But when you are big she could no longer get at me.

JaJa's mum had been furious when she found out about the assault on the teacher. It had been hard to get him into the school. It was in Dulwich, one of the nicest areas in south London, with plenty of parks and large houses. It was a few miles from Angell Town and she'd hoped that if he was at school outside the estate he wouldn't be influenced by some of the local boys. So when she got the call to say that Elijah had assaulted one of the teachers she was furious of course. She went down there and asked the teachers what happened. It was the same story she'd heard over and over again. It was Elijah's fault. She tried to defend him but no matter what she said the same answer came back. *It was Elijah's fault*.

She was even more furious when the only alternative that the education people came up with was the local school, the Lillian Bayliss School in Kennington.

One day JaJa came limping home from his new school in Kennington with blood on his trousers. He'd been stabbed in the leg.

She screamed.

'Elijah, what happened to you?'

But he wouldn't tell her. She tried again.

'Elijah, who stabbed you in the leg?'

'I've had a fight.'

She didn't believe him. She knew that it was more serious than that, but no matter how many of his friends she asked, none of them would tell her the truth.

For the next few weeks he asked for £5 to take a cab to school, rather than walk. His mum gave him the money and stopped asking questions. Secretly she believed it was that some kids had bullied Elijah into joining a gang and that he had refused.

The stabbing scared her. But fear wasn't a new emotion for her. She had always feared for Elijah. She'd been worried ever since the day that he'd been knocked over by a car while riding his bike in their local streets in Handsworth, Birmingham. He was only seven years old.

The woman driving the car ran through a red light and knocked him to the ground, breaking both his legs. It turned out later that she was drunk. When Sharon got the call about Elijah's accident she phoned her sister who lived in the same street and told her to get down there right away to find out what was going on. When her sister went out to see what was going on she too was knocked over by another driver who was rubber-necking the previous incident. By the time Sharon turned up there was chaos. Her son and her sister were both lying on the pavement with gashes to their heads and arms. When the ambulance men arrived to pick up her son, his legs swayed hideously below the knees as though it was just skin and muscle keeping them together.

From that day on we were destined for problems. Now I
worry about Elijah every single day. Every single day I
worry about him. EVERY day I worry.

She wondered how well she was bringing up her kids. She wondered whether it could have been different. Maybe if she'd
stayed in Birmingham they would have remained in their nice
home and among friends she trusted. Maybe if she'd dedicated
more time to her kids, but she'd had to take two jobs just to keep
food on the table. In the early days she'd worked at McDonalds
from 9 till 5, and made sandwiches from 7 in the evening till the
early hours of the morning. Then she would get home and while
the kids were sleeping she would wash clothes and sheets, tidy
up the house and hoover. She had to do it just to keep things in
order. She made sure that the kids had clean clothes so that when
they went out they looked good.

I remember hearing Margaret Thatcher say that she slept
for only four hours. I never slept more than four hours. I
was either out working or looking after the house or trying
to find permanent housing. It was either that or live on
social and I couldn't live on social.

She thought back to all she'd done and wondered again and again
whether she'd done her best for them. The reality was that she had
been the victim of domestic violence. That's how it had been and
that's what had set her and her kids along the path she'd taken.
She'd had no choice. She'd had to start afresh with nothing more
than five mattresses on a hostel floor. She couldn't change that
now. Now her priority was to look out for her kids.

That's why, like JaJa, Sharon used to spend time at the kitchen window, watching what was going on in Angell Town. Watching, observing and understanding. She saw the disputes going on in neighbouring council blocks; she watched the family feuds unfold. She saw the gangsters dealing drugs on the Marston House landing. One night two of them got into an argument. The shouting and cursing were so loud that she opened her door and marched up to them. She didn't care whether they had knives, guns or grenades. She'd had enough.

'Excuse me, but you cannot do your thing here. If you do, I will dub you in. I promise I will dub you in. I will go to the police and tell them who you are.'

'I'm sorry, Sharon. Don't do that. I'm really sorry but the boy was messin' with me.'

'Well, go and do your messin' somewhere else.'

The two boys went off sheepishly. Sharon Kerr heard a few days later that one of them had shot the other six times in the leg.

She'd often complained about the drug dealing and the violence to a guy from the housing department. A bald guy, who she knew as Barry, had promised them that they would get a better place outside the estate as soon as one came up. But it never happened. As far as Sharon was concerned she was trapped in Marston House and she did what she could to survive.

I didn't know London. I didn't know what to expect. I didn't know how it was going to end. We had to rough it. I had to get tough: I had to get ghetto to survive.

She softened her kids' lives by giving them their own rooms and TVs and stereos. She tried to be as open as possible with them.

She tried to let them build their own friendships. She didn't mind it when JaJa brought home friends to stay the night. Her house was open to all JaJa's friends.

I felt that nobody else cared about the kids on the estate. I was trying to give them their freedom, not be one of them rowdy Jamaican mothers, the sort that go 'You cannot come in the house, go and find something to do.' You saw a lot of those mums on the estate.

It wasn't that she believed that JaJa had too much freedom. She sometimes wondered whether she gave him enough freedom.

'Don't go out of the estate.'

That's what she'd always told him. She didn't know people beyond the Brixton road. That's why he was supposed to stay within Angell Town. She knew the Portuguese families on the estate. She knew the Africans. She knew the few white families that lived there too. In spite of the shootings, in spite of the muggings, in spite of the drug dealings and goings on, she felt Elijah was safe in Angell Town. It was one of the things she liked about Brixton. Unlike Handsworth in Birmingham where almost everyone was black, there were whites and Asians and blacks all living together in Brixton. And while she still hadn't made friends like those she'd had in Birmingham she was confident that everyone on the estate knew JaJa and would keep an eye on him.

Someone who always kept an eye on JaJa was Inch. From the balcony of Pym House, just across the way from Marston House, Inch saw what JaJa was doing. He saw the growing respect that the 28s had for JaJa. He saw JaJa's nice jeans and trainers. He saw JaJa nicking stuff and coming out with TVs from people's houses. But he wasn't yet prepared to go out by himself. He was a year younger than JaJa and not so confident.

It started slowly at first. He began to sneak out regularly to get away from his parents. Then he nicked some sweets from a sweet shop. Then he smoked a bit of weed. Once, his mum caught him with a wrap of weed that must have fallen from his pocket as he was running out of the door. He tried to explain that he didn't know what it was and where it was from. But from then on, life for Inch began to get more hectic. The more he saw JaJa doing different stuff, the more he was intrigued. Still, there was something about his upbringing that prevented him from doing more. He successfully persuaded his parents that he was innocent and hard-working, a good boy who would never get into trouble. He stuck close to Naja, JaJa's younger brother, who seemed to be quieter, calmer, less excitable than his older brother. He carried on going to church but if he received a message from someone he would sneak out, get up to some mischief and then be back in time for the final prayers. Nobody noticed he'd been gone. Inch kept behaving like a good boy. But the pressure to get the latest pair of Nike trainers was getting to him.

Chapter Nine

Back in 'the Jungle'

*Everyone was calling me the black sheep because out of all
the family I was the only one that was in bare trouble.
Trouble radiated out of me. Everyone went the right way
except for me.*

Phat Si

Fat Si had only been back in London for a few weeks and
already he was missing his mum and sisters. While he
enjoyed hanging out with JaJa and the other boys from Angell
Town he didn't feel right. He wanted to be back in Canada. The
problem was that he didn't know where his home was. He just
didn't feel good in England. He always felt like running away
and Canada was the only place he could run to. His dad didn't
seem to mind that he wanted to leave again. He bought him
another ticket back to Toronto. Fat Si was 14 years old.

His mum put him in a local school near 'the Jungle' area of
Toronto where they lived. It was mainly a Jamaican area but
there were families from all over the Caribbean. He was in the

eighth grade with his friends Calvin, Kervin, Jokes and his cousin Conrad. They formed a gang they called the Tiny Toons. His gang was made up of some other black Jamaican guys from downtown Toronto as well as a couple of Cuban and Puerto Rican guys and a Polish guy. It was a joke to start off with, horseplay, something that all kids do.

But soon the Tiny Toons were bunking off school and selling weed on the streets.

That's when it started to get serious for me. There was drugs and guns around. Bare guns. Bare guns – street talk for lots of guns.

Then Fat Si got involved with one of his relatives. The relative asked Fat Si to help him push drugs on the street. It started with weed but soon he was pushing a new drug that he'd heard about but hadn't really paid much attention to. Crack cocaine had been around for nearly a decade on the streets of Toronto and Fat Si knew that the money he could earn was much greater. He started learning. He knew that his relative got his rocks of crack from a dealer who took cocaine powder, mixed it with water and sodium bicarbonate and heated it over hot water, dissolving the liquid until it turned into small rocks of cocaine. It was called crack because of the sound it made as it dissolved. One day he stole into his relative's apartment and looked for the hiding place.

I knew where he'd put it. I thought, 'I'm gonna tief a piece.' Steal it. I cut off a piece and went out and sold it. Then I did it again and again.

But the money he got from dealing was never enough.

One evening he saw a Filipino guy walking along the street by himself. Fat Si didn't plan it but he knew he wanted money. He was broke so he just jumped him.

I don't know what happened. I felt kinda bad afterwards. Much later. I was big and I just grabbed him by his collar and went through his pockets.

'Gimme your money.'

He went through the Filipino's jacket and pulled out a wallet. It contained about $140. He took the loose notes and the loose change too and left with the guy's pager. He didn't feel bad at the time. He thought it was funny. He went and bought a bottle of Bacardi lemon from a local liquor store.

He began to live a mad, hectic life. He stayed out late, drinking alcohol in the park, smoking weed and showing off to the girls.

They loved my accent, I was different and I wasn't posh with it as well. I was from the ghetto and that and I was streetwise and I could have a tear up. I could fight and that. I always got girls. They wanted to be around me all the time. All sorts of girls would go for me, black, Guyanese, Jamaican, African, Puerto Rican, Hungarian, Filipino. They loved me.

He stopped going to school, started smoking crack and got an exhilarating buzz from feeling that he was living on the edge.

To stop himself from going nuts he partied even harder. Then he got his girlfriend pregnant. He was 15.

He didn't know she was pregnant at the time. She was called Lisa Muswell and she was from Trinidad. She was beautiful. The first time Fat Si saw her he liked her. He was already fucking a girl called Karen, but he was just fucking her, not going with her. When he saw Lisa Muswell that all changed. He spent a year just hanging out with her. He didn't want to kiss her. He just wanted to be with her, to 'roll' with her. A year and a half after meeting her he realized how much he liked her.

But then he got stabbed.

His gang had been in the train station having a ruck with another gang. Fat Si had got the better of one of their guys but three days later they came for their revenge.

He was on his way with Giddy and Geoff, a Colombian friend, to visit a white girl called Kerry. They planned to smoke some weed together. They had just stepped out of the elevator and were walking along the hallway of her apartment block when the elevator opened again and six guys came out. The bigger guy spoke first.

'Which one was it?'

The guy Fat Si had beaten up pointed at him.

'That's him.'

Then they just jumped on him. Fat Si fought and fought until he heard someone speak.

'That's enough, put it away.'

Fat Si had no idea what that meant. He felt nothing. The girl opened the door and started screaming. There was blood everywhere. Fat Si had no idea that it was him who was bleeding. His friends bundled him into a car and they took him to hospital.

The knife had punctured Fat Si's lung. His first thought was of all the trouble he was causing his mum. His second thought was of betrayal.

> *I thought I'd been set up. I wondered whether it had been the girl Kerry. From a young age, ever since I was a kid, people have always snaked me and sold me down the river. I don't know what it is. Now I'm trying to break the cycle. D'you get me?*

A month later he was arrested for robbery and sent away. His mum couldn't cope with him any more. He was skinny now and drawn out. She had a go at him.

'You can't stay here.'

His bail condition was that he had to go and live in the mainly white suburb of Mississauga, where his grandmother did foster work. It was an hour away from Toronto so he couldn't see Lisa. He missed her and all his friends.

The good thing was that for a while he cleaned up his life. He broke his leg and was on crutches which kept him in High School for a while. But there were some kids there who knew he was from Toronto and knew of his reputation so he started selling weed again. The school finally had enough and kicked him out. Then some of the foster kids got into trouble because of him. His family thought that he was nothing but trouble. They began to treat him as the black sheep of the family. He was the only one who was having such problems. His stepbrother was on his way to becoming an NBA basketball player and his sisters were doing OK. Yet he was always getting arrested. He went back to Toronto to see if he could sort his life out but he was arrested for robbery again. He'd gone into a shop, jumped the counter and taken money from the till.

The youth court at 311 Jarvis Street in downtown Toronto sent him to a detention centre where, for four weeks, he slept in a big dormitory with other young offenders and played basketball and lifted weights. The other guys on the wing were black guys from out of state so they got on OK. He built himself up until he was all brawn and muscle. The bail condition was that he could go back to Mississauga but if he was caught in a criminal act over the next fifteen months it was serious. He would go to prison.

His family had had enough of him.

As soon as she could, his grandmother put him on a plane back to England.

Chapter Ten

Ribz

I thought I could do things differently, but where I messed up was from school. Like I never went to school. Where I used to see things so much like my mum getting hit and my brothers going through madness it kind of messed with my head, so when I was in school it wasn't to learn, it was to muck about really.

Ribz

'Electric Avenue', Eddie Grant's summer hit about Brixton, was playing on the radio when Ribz, or Byron Cole as he was more properly known, came into the world.

Now in the streets there is violence,
And a lot of work to be done…
We're gonna rock down to, Electric Avenue,
And then we'll take it higher…

It was 1983, and on the streets of south London tension and

resentment against the police were still high. The police had
not managed to make any major inroads into improving community relations in south-west London since the riots two years
earlier. Brixton was still on the brink of violence.

Byron's earliest memory was of his mum coming home one day to
the house in Union Road in Stockwell where he lived with his
two older brothers, Errol and Kojo. She was carrying lots of
packages. His first thought was that she must be going on holiday.
He was four years old.

   His next memory is of being woken up early one morning
by the sound of shouting and crashing. The door opened and a
team of police officers burst in and searched the house. As they
led his mother away in handcuffs they told the young Byron
Cole that the packages his mum had brought home contained
heroin and crack cocaine. She was storing them and selling them
on to various dealers. He didn't really know what any of it
meant but soon after that it was downhill all the way for Byron
Cole. His mum was sent to prison for pushing drugs and Byron
was sent into care. His dad was already in prison so there was
no one to look after him. And anyway, he didn't really know
who his dad was. He had a memory of visiting a man in prison
who they said was his dad.

> *I must have been about seven. I'll never forget it. It's like
> bored in the back of my mind. I can always remember going
> in and seeing him.*

The man picked him up and showed him round proudly to the
other inmates.

'This is my son.'

That was the last time Byron ever saw him.

The foster care home was a couple of miles from Angell Town. He was sent there with his brother Kojo. Byron was now five years old. It wasn't a happy time. The woman who fostered them had kids of her own but used to take her anger out on Byron and his brother. It was Byron and Kojo who suffered whenever her own kids did something wrong. Sometimes she would hit Byron with a broom handle or a stick. She'd lash out at him with a shoe or whatever else she had to hand. Sometimes she'd slap him and he'd run upstairs to the bedroom he shared with his brother and hide under the bed. It wouldn't matter whether they had done anything wrong or whether it was Byron's fault or Kojo's fault; they would both get a beating.

> *Sometimes she'd hit me for no reason when she was mad. If my brother done something wrong I'd get beat. If I'd done something wrong, he'd get the blame. We never used to get beat separate. When she had an outburst with her family she was more likely to take it out on you because you are nothing.*

The woman's kids were always up to no good, hanging around outside the front gate. Byron would watch from his bedroom window as groups of older kids would turn up out of the blue, skulking by the front gate, as though they didn't want to be seen. The woman's son and daughter would disappear into the house and come back with something and hand it to some of those hanging round outside. His brother told him that the woman's kids and nephews were dealing in drugs outside the foster home. Even though he was still very young, Byron had an understanding of what was going on. He'd seen it with his mother. He also knew that those who dealt drugs would generally use them. He'd seen that with his mother too.

Even though it was obvious to Byron what was going on, the woman who ran the foster home didn't seem to care what was happening outside her front gate. He thought she was turning a blind eye.

> *If I know what was going on, I guess she knew what was going on. No matter what, she got paid. She'd qualified to foster kids so she didn't care. At the end of the day she was getting paid. Not all carers are perfect, I can tell you that.*

When his mother came out of prison on home leave and heard what was going on in Tulse Hill she got permission to take him out of there. She sent him to live with his nan in Tooting Bec.

His nan was fine. But Byron wasn't happy. *What was I expected to do in the house of an old person?* What he really wanted was to be with his mum. So when his mum finally came out of prison he was overjoyed. They moved back into Union Road and life returned to some sort of normality. For a couple of weeks anyway.

Byron was now eight years old. That's when he started robbing. At first it was just sweets from the newsagents. Then it was clothes and trainers.

When he turned nine, he started mugging other kids and old ladies on Union Road and running away with their purses and handbags.

A few months later, the family, such as it was, moved to a new place. They drove up Stockwell Road towards Brixton and got housing in a council block called Pym House on an estate called Angell Town. But it didn't help much. His mum still did drugs and had boyfriends that were into the wrong sort of stuff. Some of the neighbours in the new place complained about the Cole family, saying that they were a bad lot and that Angell Town was turning into a 'sink estate'. There were allegations doing the rounds of the estate that the Lambeth housing authorities were dumping problem families in Angell Town.

It's true that Byron's older brothers were going through problems. All of his family, his brothers, his mother, his mother's boyfriends were involved in certain things: robbing and shotting (selling drugs) and mugging. It all happened in front of Byron's eyes. That's all he ever knew.

But the worst thing was seeing his mum get beaten up over and over again by the various boyfriends who used to walk in and out of the flat. That really messed with his head.

A year after moving into Pym House, Byron heard loud bangs. He was out and about on the estate. It was just after 5 November and he thought the noises were fireworks. But when he got home to Pym House he saw ambulances gathered round the entrance to his flat. His stepfather had been shot in the leg and had jumped off the balcony into the garden below. He ran upstairs and told his mum what had happened. Somewhere, deep down, he knew he should have been surprised by seeing someone getting shot outside his house but he had already seen so much that it didn't really register with him. Not much registered with Byron. In fact, while other kids seemed to run around in the streets hollering and having fun, or kicking a football on the Angell Town football pitch, Byron lived his life in a sort of numbed, insipid haze.

Whether it was the numbness that prevented him from making friends or the lack of friends that caused the numbness, he didn't know. Whatever it was, Byron was a loner. He had his brothers around him every now and then but he never had any real friends. His brother had got to know a couple of older kids on the estate and they treated him well enough. One of them was called Elijah and he had recently arrived on the estate from Birmingham. Elijah used to hang out with the older kids and would sometimes make a point of checking on Byron and giving him money. Byron looked up to the kid from Birmingham. He felt there was some unusual kindness in him that he didn't notice in other people on the estate very often. Everyone called the older boy from Birmingham, JaJa.

Chapter Eleven

A New Coldness

It was like a new coldness had come into the estate. Before it was all about peace and unity. Now it was disputes and guns and knives.

Pod

So many shootings were taking place in Angell Town that few remembered exactly when they all started. Pod, though, would never forget the first shooting he saw. It was etched on his mind. It was a year or so before the 28s were formed. He'd just turned 15.

It happened in the playground area sandwiched between Pym House and Marston House. It was a shoot-out, a turf war between two Yardie groups from Jamaica. One crew was from Spanish Town, the other from Kingston. Each group wanted exclusive rights over the drug dealing in Angell Town. They confronted each other during the day while little kids were playing on the swings and pushing each other on the rusty roundabout. It started with raised voices, then yelling, then shots rang out, scattering everyone in all directions. Pod saw little kids trying to get out of the way of the flying bullets.

I realized that life on Angell Town had moved to another level. I was scared that the moment had come when Angell Town began to go downhill.

It was about a year later when there was a second event on the estate. He was hanging around Pym House with a friend when a black man in ragged clothes came in and started walking around the estate. It was unusual. Outsiders didn't usually come into the estate. Especially not late at night. Especially not alone.

A lot of people couldn't really come into the area. They have to know someone. To walk into Angell Town was scary and we in the 28s would be there and it would be bottles and stones to get them out of Angell Town.

Pod's friend got ready to chase the stranger out of the estate. He and Pod began to taunt the man.

'Hey, get out of our area.'

Then Pod's friend ran up to the man and gave him a good kicking.

The bloke ran off but as he went he turned round menacingly.

'I'll be back.'

Half an hour later, just as it started to rain, the same figure appeared again, this time dressed in a long black Yardie-style coat.

Pod was waiting for him, this time with some of the 28s who had gathered underneath Pym House. They were about to taunt the stranger again when he suddenly pulled out a long sword from under his coat and began to swing it wildly around his head. He caught Pod on the arms and legs, slashing holes in his coat and slicing his skin.

One of Pod's friends, who went by the street name of Shortdust, was caught up in the mêlée. As he tried to get away he slipped on the rubber matting that covered the ground around Pym House. The sword-wielding maniac came at him, slicing his head as Shortdust cowered on the ground.

The 28s rushed at the maniac until finally they managed to chase him off.

Pod and Shortdust were taken to hospital with severe cuts to their heads, arms and legs. Their injuries were so severe that the story appeared on the local news.

They never saw the man again.

The incident shocked Pod. His earliest memories of the Yardies in Angell Town had been positive. As a kid he'd looked up to them as they swaggered into Angell Town decked out in gold jewellery and long, flowing coats topped off with their colourful dread berets. They were the ones who organized top reggae artists to come over from Jamaica to play on the estate. They had respect and prestige. But now the relationship was beginning to sour. The Yardies had always been in charge of selling drugs on the block. But things were changing. The British-born gang members wanted the turf for themselves and resented the presence of the Yardies.

As we got older we never respected them as much. Some of
the originals, those who had been there a long time, we left

alone, but the new Yardies we never got on with. They used
to try and intimidate us.

The clashes would begin when some of the Yardies would
approach the 28s as they were hanging around the block.

'Come off the block. Don't come round here.'

The Yardies complained that the 28s were stopping their
business.

The 28s, though, refused to move.

We couldn't take that so we would fight them off. They
couldn't do nothing and we were always going to give
trouble so they left us alone but after that we never was
tight with the Yardies.

It was around this time that Pod noticed another little kid
hanging around the fringes of the Younger 28s. The kid was
always riding around on his BMX bike seeing what the older
boys like Elijah Kerr were up to. There was something lonely
about the kid. He didn't seem to have many friends. Pod
noticed how he struggled. He was having to make a life for
himself. He realized that the kid was the younger brother of
the two Cole brothers, Kojo and Errol. He learnt his name was
Byron. Everyone on the estate, including Pod, knew that their
mother was never around because she was either in prison or
out of her head in some crack den.

Pod felt protective towards the boy and tried to encourage
him. He knew that a lot of the kids on the estate, including some
of the 28s, didn't have fathers.

*The 28s would protect the younger guys. The 28s were role
models and we tried to be role models for each other. It's like
fathering each other. Some of our parents couldn't parent us
so if we tiefed a packet of crisps we would share it round.
There was never a day that someone would be hungry.*

He knew that the Younger 28s like JaJa and Fat Si and Inch
would be the next generation and it was important to teach them
something, even if it meant that some of the 28s taught them how
to make money from drugs and robbing. With Byron he took
extra special care. He felt that there was a vulnerability about the
kid. That's why he urged his father, Pastor Samuels, Angell
Town's preacher, to invite Byron and kids like him round on a
Sunday to feed them a slap-up meal of chicken, rice and peas.

*I thought if no one looks after him he'll be homeless or go
mental or something. Kids like that didn't have family and
some of us didn't so that's why we used to call each other 'cus'
or 'cousin'. We weren't family but we almost acted like we
were.*

It was on 20 July 1994 that the 'family' suffered its first serious
loss, and it affected those in the 28s for years afterwards.

It was a Wednesday evening and Perry, one of the biggest
names in the 28s, had just dropped Pod off in Angell Town.
Perry was a role model for kids on the estate. He held down a
steady job as a photocopying engineer yet most evenings he
would still be found in jeans and a baseball cap having fun with
the rest of the 28s. That evening he planned to go street racing

in Camberwell with Wesley and Drops, twin brothers who were also key members of the Angell Town gang.

It wasn't until next morning that the news reached Angell Town. Perry and the twins had been racing through south-east London when Perry had lost control of the car and driven at high speed into a skip. Perry and Wesley died almost instantly. Drops, Wesley's twin brother, was taken to hospital with broken ribs and serious concussion.

The funeral was the biggest event ever to happen in Angell Town. The whole estate knew them and over a thousand turned out for the procession. Once the hearses had gone and the bouquets of flowers had been taken away, the sound systems came out around the estate's football pitch. To the sound of reggae music, the community mourned the death of two of their own.

It was the end of an era. The 28s were never the same force after that. And besides, a new generation was waiting in the wings. Lining the street, looking on in awe at the flower-covered black cars that crawled silently through the estate, were a bunch of younger kids who were ready to usurp the 28s as the most important gang on the estate.

Chapter Twelve

Steaming

This was a new thing. It was called 'steaming'. We just run in, knock the bloke over, usually a little Indian guy who is scared, coz we were big black guys, hats low over our faces, hungry for money, looking like proper criminals. We'd jump the counter, get to the cash register and smash it down on the ground. And then one of the big boys told us an easier way. They said just press the N/S key and it opens. Ching! Sometimes we'd get £1,000 like that.

JaJa

Sharon Kerr's fears for her son turned out to be well founded. JaJa's change of school from Dulwich to Kennington opened up another world to him. Another criminal world. It was the summer of 1995, and a fellow member of the Younger 28s told him about a new way of getting money. He called it 'steaming'. JaJa learnt quickly.

We went to a shop in Brixton and ran in there and steamed the place. Hundreds of people were doing it. It started with two of us at first and then everyone heard about it and we linked up after school and did it. We were the Younger 28s and we all did it together, all the little ones together, younger cousins and that. We all went out there robbing and steaming places. It was happening for a year straight. And then that got too easy.

It started with newsagents. They would run in en masse and take what they could from the till. Then they graduated to larger shops.

There were police chases in and out of Angell Town that JaJa and his friends found exhilarating. But they were hardly ever caught because they knew all the alleys and passageways they could use to escape. Even if they were arrested they were so young that they got bail straightaway. It was a pain having to go to a probation officer and do community service, but the inconvenience was easily dwarfed by the excitement of having money to spend on trainers and new clothes. JaJa and the Younger 28s became more ambitious. They started on banks and building societies. Sometimes they would be able to get away with five grand. For the next twelve months, JaJa and his gang travelled around London steaming banks and building societies. The technique was the same as they'd used on newsagents. They would turn up en masse and rush the bank counter and pull out whatever they could. Life was different then. There was no security glass and no security guards to stop them. It was easy.

JaJa was now 16 years old. Life was mad and heavy.

Gangsta rap was all the rage on the streets of Brixton. Snoop Doggy Dogg, Biggie Smalls, Dr Dre and Tupac Shakur rapped about 'bitches' and 'hos' or whores. In 'Cop Killer', Ice T rapped about guns, violence and hatred of the police. JaJa could feel that his body was changing, almost to the beat of the music.

It started with an excess of energy and frustration. He began to smoke crack. The taste was different from weed, and instead of making him feel chilled it livened him up. The taste was sweet. One puff and he immediately felt the effect. His eyes opened wider, he stood taller, he felt more alive. He put all his energy into robbing.

He put the wads of notes that he collected under his bed, in a shoebox.

I was just robbing and causing chaos. It was wild and crazy. It was nuts. I didn't care. I was going through teenage years and things start happening and everything came at me at once. And the only way for us to handle that was to take our frustration out on society and we were broke and we put all our energy into robbing. That was like play-time and money-time, everything rolled in one. We weren't scared. It was a joke. It was like a big adventure.

Sharon Kerr, JaJa's mum, was working so hard that she didn't completely realize what was going on. When she got back late at night, she would put on the reggae she liked. Her daughters would be in their rooms listening to their own reggae. JaJa and his friends, Inch, Birdie and Solomon Martin who went by the street name of Blacker, would be in his bedroom, listening to Tupac and Biggie, the heavy rap beat thumping out of his room. She didn't mind. What went on in his room was his business. She was pleased that JaJa always had a lot of people around him.

> *Elijah was a child who was born a leader ever since he was*
> *a baby. I don't know how to explain Elijah. He draws*
> *people around him and they expect him to lead. He's always*
> *had these different age people around him.*

She had no idea of the money accumulating in the shoebox under JaJa's bed.

Then one day, a weekday, very early in the morning there was a banging on the door.

'Police. Open up.'

The next thing she knew was that several policemen broke down her door with a small battering ram and began to search the house.

'Where's Elijah Kerr's bedroom?'

They searched the whole house but didn't find anything. Not even the shoebox.

And then it happened again. And again.

It was always the same old story. They were looking for Elijah and trying to find money, crack, weed, guns. They never did find anything but still they kept searching.

After a few months they were so used to the whole process that they began to call her by her first name.

'Sharon. You know why we are here. We're looking for Elijah.'

They got to know the layout of the family flat, whose rooms belonged to whom. Soon they were raiding the house about once a month. Sharon's low opinion of the police fell even lower. *It was a game for them. It was all just routine.*

They never did find anything and got more and more irritated. They knew that she was protecting him.

And it was true. Sharon always tried to cover for her son no matter what. But there was only so much she was prepared to take. She took JaJa aside one day.

'I can't do this no more. It's got to stop. It's becoming harassment.'

'I know.'

That was all JaJa could say.

But it didn't stop. And while Sharon would always protect him, she never really knew exactly what she was protecting him from. Her policy was not to ask too much. She knew that there were drug dealers operating out of the council blocks. She knew that there were guns and knives around. She knew that the Yardies and the 28s robbed and mugged. She knew that these were all bad influences for her boys. But she never really knew exactly what JaJa was doing out in the street. And she never really wanted to know.

It wasn't just her boys she was worried about. The estate was just as bad for the girls as for the boys.

It was the vulnerable girls who got into problems. Sharon often stood at her window overlooking Angell Town, watching the Yardies at work. Even though she thought of herself as 'a tough mama' she found the big black men operating outside her door scary. She knew what was going on. She knew that some of the girls got into drink and drugs and then got kidnapped and locked in flats or in the garages under the blocks. The next thing she would hear was that some of the men were raping them repeatedly. But everyone knew who the rapists and the bad ones were.

She put some of the blame on the mums on the estate. Sometimes they were as bad as the girls. They too were on the drink or on drugs and turned a blind eye to the goings-on. But Sharon made sure she told her daughters of the dangers.

'Stay away from that one. He's a rapist.'

From the balcony she would point out to her daughters the men they should stay away from.

'Careful. He will drag you off.'

She blamed the government for letting all the people from Jamaica into the country. British black were different from Yardie black and African black. *Why we get put in one group, I don't know. We are all different cultures.* It meant that Sharon never really felt she belonged in Britain. And she never belonged in Jamaica either. In Britain people called her 'Jamaican'. But when she went to Jamaica to see relatives, the locals would shout at her in the streets: 'Hey, English'.

Chantelle, Sharon's oldest daughter and JaJa's younger sister, would listen to her mum's worries and try and placate her. She too had heard the stories on the street and made sure she stayed away from the bad men. But she was bold and it didn't stop her from a young age going down the 'block' at night and hanging around with the Yardies and the English black boys. She would chat with them and get money from them. The Yardies didn't care. They'd just hand out a few notes.

She began to watch JaJa going out at night. He wouldn't tell her at first what he was doing but she found his lifestyle intriguing and exciting.

It was different for girls. She and her sister were supposed to stay at home. They never quite got in the same trouble as the boys. Little things, yes, but Chantelle never got into as much trouble with the police as JaJa.

When her mum wasn't around, she and her sister used to find JaJa on the estate and run errands for him.

'Chantelle, go and look down there. Go, look, see if there are any feds. See if anything is going on.'

Fascinated, and fuelled by the intrigue, she would run along the pedways and see whether the coast was clear. Then she would run back with the news.

'No feds around.'

Sometimes she would follow JaJa and others in the Younger 28s. Chantelle and her friends wanted to get involved so badly. They used to pester JaJa if he was planning to do some robbery.

'Girls would be better than boys at it.'

But JaJa would never let them.

He was protecting us, I guess. If I was a boy I'd definitely be doing it as well. Instead of letting us get involved, Elijah used to hand out money. We never had to ask.

Then one day it went wrong for Elijah Kerr. He and his gang had gone to Bromley in Kent to steam a Nationwide building society. JaJa was on lookout as some of the Younger 28s pulled masks over their faces and rushed at the counter. They came away with bags of money in their arms. But as they stepped out of the premises the sirens started wailing. Suddenly there were police everywhere. Most of them got nicked straightaway. JaJa anticipated what was going on and made a run for it. He ran down Bromley High Street and into the side streets where they had parked their hire car. He was relieved when he got there. But as he went to open the car door, the shouting began.

'Get down, Elijah. Face down on the floor.'

Undercover cops had tracked them all the way from Brixton.

JaJa and the others were put in holding cells at Orpington police station for three days. He got bailed to appear in court. JaJa didn't mind. He thought it was a joke.

Sharon didn't see the funny side. Yet again, there was a knock on the door.

'Police. Open up.'

It was the fifth raid in a couple of weeks. This time the police cleaned out the house. They took the TVs, videos and music systems. They took away JaJa's clothes and trainers as evidence. They wanted to know how he had managed to obtain so many designer clothes and so much expensive music equipment. Suddenly, instead of dealing with the local police in Brixton, Sharon was dealing with police as far away as Orpington in Kent. Over the course of a year she got so many calls to take JaJa fresh clothes or money to various police stations in Essex or Kent that she no longer knew which police force she was dealing with.

For JaJa the whole thing was still like a big adventure. At Bromley Crown Court the judge took a look at his long criminal record.

'You're not getting bail today; you are getting a custodial sentence for this crime.'

JaJa couldn't believe it. He was only 16 years old.

'What?'

The judge gave him three years. The solicitor told him that he'd only have to do half the sentence and that he'd be out in 18 months.

I couldn't stop thinking about it. I'm not coming out until the summer of 1998. No way. You can't be serious. I'll be old. No way. Then my head started spinning.

Chapter Thirteen

Birdie

I was playing with fire and I was getting away with it. D'you get me? From then on, I knew I didn't want to go to jail. Everyone else was going to jail and they were proud of it. I was never like that. I started thinking before I done anything.

Birdie

Birdie, like Inch, was a year younger than JaJa, and although he knew what JaJa was up to he stayed away from the steaming and the house burglaries. Birdie just did his own thing, watching JaJa go further and further afield for his thieving exploits. Birdie and JaJa were different. They looked different and acted different. Birdie was smaller, more lithe, more unassuming than JaJa, who radiated a restless energy. It was something that Birdie admired in his friend. *That JaJa is a wanderer.* Birdie preferred to stay closer to home. And JaJa, although he lived next door and they saw each other every day, never pushed Birdie into it. In fact, Birdie thought that JaJa respected him for not following what all the other Younger 28s were doing.

Not that Birdie was all innocent. His mum had sent him to school in Victoria to get him away from the bad influences in Brixton and Angell Town. He went to the Westminster City School and most of the kids there were white. But its distance from Angell Town didn't help. By December of his first year he and ten others had got suspended for shoplifting at the Army and Navy store on Victoria Street. The police said they'd caught them on videotape. Most of the other boys who were caught were in tears. They were crying and they were scared. But not Birdie. He'd watched JaJa going in and out of youth court and knew what it was all about.

A couple of years later, though, it got more serious. It was during a music lesson. The music teacher used to come in, give them some books and then go off and have a smoke in his room. While he was out, Birdie and the others started flicking pieces of paper wrapped in a flammable liquid that they'd picked up in chemistry. It got out of hand and the flames burned some guy's jacket. The boy told the teacher and there was a big investigation. Even though everyone was involved it was always Birdie's name that kept coming up as the main instigator.

When his mum got the letter telling her that he was permanently excluded she was furious and grounded him. Birdie felt persecuted. What made him most furious was when he found out that, of the twenty statements given to the headmaster, eighteen of them had his name on. That's not what happened in Angell Town.

Everyone put the blame on me, but I wasn't the only one. Where I come from you don't grass anyone up. In Angell Town no one ever snakes.

103

In the end his mum appealed and they let him back. But it didn't stop there. They put him in a different form to split him up from the other troublemakers. The problem was that he had now acquired a reputation. He was from Brixton and the other kids thought he was cool and wanted to hang out with him. He decided to do things smartly. He stayed out of trouble by getting the younger kids to do things for him so that he wouldn't be seen to be the main man. If he saw trouble ahead he would back off, kick back and chill.

It worked. For a time, anyway.

One day Birdie and some of his schoolmates went to hang out at a rival school in Pimlico. It was a mixed school and they wanted to meet some girls. When they got there they found that the school kids in Pimlico had nice clothes and money to buy their lunch from a nearby pizza place. Birdie never had money to buy pizza at school. He thought it was unfair. They went over to some of the kids and lined them up against a wall.

'Listen. What have you got in your pockets?'

He and his mates threatened the Pimlico kids until they paid up. They made them empty their pockets. Sometimes they made off with £30 or £40. It lasted a couple of weeks. One lunchtime they saw a police van outside the Pimlico school. They ran back to their own school in Victoria but there was a police van there too outside the school gates. They tried to run and mingle with the passers-by on Victoria Street but the police caught up with them and nicked them. In the end the boys' parents didn't want the hassle of pressing charges so the case was dropped. But it had scared Birdie. He decided then and there that if he robbed or did something wrong again he would never get caught.

Chapter Fourteen

Feltham

I look back now and see that it made me grow up quicker. I was only 16 and I had time to think and read more. You start realizing that you are by yourself. It forces you to act older. At the same time it makes you miss out on a lot of things. That can turn you crazy. Loads of nights I was thinking, 'I shouldn't be here. What am I doing here?' It's wasting time.

JaJa

A big cage. That's what JaJa thought of the place. He was 16 when he began his first custodial sentence for steaming the building society in Bromley. He was sent to Feltham, a young offenders' institution in Middlesex. He was horrified when he saw the barbed wire on the red-brick perimeter walls and the iron bars and gates in Feltham's corridors.

But once inside he found that he was with friends from all over south London. There were friends he'd known from Angell Town, friends who'd been nicked for some of the robberies he'd also done in Peckham and Clapham and Stockwell. It was like a meeting place for all those he'd gone out robbing with. Not that he got a lot of time with them. He was banged up by himself for twenty-three hours a day, six months straight, with no TV, just a small radio and an hour to do exercise and have a shower. His cell was cold, smelly and grotty and the bed was dirty. To pass the time he amused himself by banging on the pipes and shouting to the neighbouring cell.

'Hey, you, where you from?'

'I'm from Streatham. Where you from?'

'I'm from Angell Town. Who's in the cell next to you?'

They could keep up the constant banging and yelling for days, even though the staff told them to shut up. He obsessed about the two years he still had to serve. The noise and knowledge that he had friends in the cells next door just about made it bearable.

After six months he was told he was going to move. A van came and took him to Aylesbury in Buckinghamshire. There he got to work in the prison kitchens. He was allowed to take woodwork and other education classes. His day was spent going to classes, having lunch, then working in the kitchens until the evening when he'd get two hours off before lights out. Being busy at least made the sentence easier to handle.

But it didn't stop the painful thoughts that had started in Feltham from coming back each night. Some nights, the thoughts that popped into his head made him turn crazy. He realized he was wasting his life. That time was short. He stopped the thoughts by grabbing any book he could.

I read Jackie Collins, Sidney Sheldon, Wilbur Smith, the Bible. Action books, fantasy books, even romance books. It

was the first time I'd read a whole book to the end.
Whatever book I could get, I read. I'm good at reading. I
was good at school, my work was good, not good at maths
but otherwise I was good. I had top-notch writing. I was
thinking life sucks. I was thinking I've got to better myself
when I get out. I've got to up my game.

He began to make plans for what he was going to do when he got
back to Angell Town. He decided that he wasn't going to get
sucked back into a life of crime. In his head he dreamt of setting
up a music business. He formulated plans for organizing raves.
He worked out which venues he would hire, how he would get
hold of artists and DJs, how he was going to market the raves.
Day after day he began to plan it, obsessively. He listened to Tim
Westwood's music show on Radio 1 and got hold of tapes and
CDs of rap music. Before long, in his head, he was at the top of
the music business with his raves and rap events taking place all
across the country. He looked around for inspiration. He knew of
a friend of his from school who he'd also been out robbing with.
He too was in prison. He didn't know the guy that well. They
hadn't clicked at school but JaJa wanted to run his ideas past him.
They started writing to each other, telling each other about the
sort of music that was out there and making plans for the future.
The friend kept signing off his letters with the initials PDC. JaJa
was intrigued. He wanted to know more. The friend was
Jamaican and he seemed to know his music. His street name was
Bloods.

Chapter Fifteen

Bloods

'Course I could get guns. We could all get 'straps' or 'burners'. I'd make a call and get a gun. Whatever I wanted. Let's just leave it at that. I kept a black .38 tucked into my waistband.

Bloods

It was Bloods who first came up with the name PDC. It was 1995 and he was in a car with a couple of his friends, Arch and Drum, and his 'cousin' who went by the street name of Jonny Peelo. They were driving through Stockwell on their way to do a robbery. Smoking and robbing and listening to music. That's how they lived. They travelled around south London doing 'stick-ups'. They drove around with guns, threatening drug dealers, and running into bars and shops, waving guns around. They were 'stick-up kids'. That evening they were listening to ragga music on the car stereo. They didn't like hip-hop. They preferred the harsh, rude, violent lyrics of ragga, like Elephant Man, Bounty Killer and the Scare Dem Crew.

Bad man ah Bad man, Ah we no rob man,
ohh bad man no freak man,
Gunshot ah beat man,
bad man no support caine.

Bloods turned to his 'cousin'.

'We are the Peel Dem Crew.'

The others in the car thought it was funny. It was a good description. They 'peeled' things from people. It was Jamaican street talk for robbing, stealing.

The name stuck after that. There were only four of them and they were only young but they already had a gang name. It gave them a separate identity from the older boys they used to hang around with, guys who called themselves the 28s. Even though Bloods was only 15 he felt that he and his crew had gone up in the world. PDC. The Peel Dem Crew. It sounded good.

Bloods had been born in the last days of 1979 in Kingston, Jamaica. Few people knew his birth name and he preferred it like that. Even 'Bloods' was one of several street names he used to keep his identity secret from the police and rivals or enemies on the street. He'd come over to England when he was six years old with his mum, his older brother and his uncle. His dad was already living in Brixton and had found them a squat on an estate called Angell Town.

For the next three years, the five of them lived in the squat in a council block called Ireton House, next to another block called Marston House.

Bloods hated the place, mostly because the house he had grown up in in Jamaica was bigger, sunnier and airier. You could fit twenty of the Ireton House flats in his old house in Jamaica. While he hated the flat, he didn't mind the estate. It was different, a new environment with an interesting vibe, so he made the most of it. And there were lots of kids on the estate to hang out with.

Bloods didn't stay long in Angell Town. He kept getting into trouble so his family sent him to Birmingham to live with his grandparents. He misbehaved there too and was rude and did 'dumb shit'. During the summer his grandparents were relieved when he went back to London to spend the holidays with the rest of his family who had just moved to Minet Road, on the edge of Angell Town. That's how he ended up hanging around with the older guys and their gangs. His brother had joined the Untouchables. His uncle and his cousin were in the 28s. In the house where he lived there were members of rival gangs living under the same roof. In such a close-knit community they all had to get along, and Bloods, with a foot in each camp, managed to straddle the two gangs. It couldn't last. Bloods was drawn to one gang. That's how he ended up 'spa-ing' or hanging out with some of the Jamaican guys who had been taken in by the 28s. That's how he got mixed up in the Yardie crowd. That's how he learned about drugs and mugging and 'tiefing'.

When he was 11, Bloods's parents allowed him to move back to London for good. They thought that, now he was older, he might be easier to control. They had moved across the Brixton Road into a house in Stockwell. But he was sent to a school in Putney. His parents thought it would stop him hanging out with the bad sorts who used to hang around Angell Town. It didn't stop him. It made it worse. In Putney he 'bumped' school, started smoking weed and selling the stuff too. He robbed and mugged using techniques he'd learnt from the Yardie crowd. That ranged from distracting someone and snatching a handbag, to smashing a car window and running off with the car stereo. He would do anything he could to get hold of money. He had two friends, one called Mutley and the other called Mac who, although he was only 13 or 14, looked as though he was in his 20s. He was fucking a girl who worked behind the counter of a local jewellery shop. One lunchtime she came up with a suggestion.

'Take whatever you want.'

So one evening she opened up the shop and Bloods and Mutley took all the jewellery they could lay their hands on. It was too easy.

It didn't take long before his teachers grew tired of his constant truancy and misbehaving at school. He was thrown out and moved to the Lillian Bayliss School in Kennington. It was there that he met a new kid, a kid called Elijah who had also grown up in Birmingham. Everyone called him JaJa. Bloods liked him. He was a cool guy, but they weren't best friends. He was a big guy, a good foot taller than Bloods. He wasn't a troublemaker but Bloods could tell he could look after himself. *If you crossed him he could fuck you up.*

Then his mum died. He was 15. His mum had cancer. His dad called him from the hospital.

'Your mum is dead.'

Bloods went numb. He was numb for a day, then two days, then a week. He stayed at home. He didn't want to see anyone. Then one day there was a knock on the door.

It was Elijah.

'I heard your mum passed. I came to see how you are.'

For the next few days, JaJa and another friend called Mikey used to come round and see him, checking that he was OK. It was something that Bloods never forgot. From then on he treated JaJa with respect. Even when JaJa did something he didn't like, Bloods would forgive him.

I am very sentimental with people. You could do the smallest thing and I would hold it in my heart forever. If you do bad things I most probably won't bring no harm to you, because of that small thing you've done. I'll be upset with you. But I won't bring no harm to you.

For weeks, Bloods withdrew. He was quiet and pensive. Then he went wild.

He started getting hold of guns and doing 'stick-ups' and bank robberies. He was friends with all the Yardie men. He could call any of them and get whatever weapon he wanted. He kept a .38 revolver tucked into his waistband and went out on the road. He would get high and go with Jonny Peelo to the Peckham 'frontline' where the drug dealers were and find some guy who was selling drugs on the street.

'I need some gear.'

'Come with me.'

When the dealer took him to a quiet place Bloods would get out the .38 and put the cold barrel to the dealer's temple.

'Give me your money or I'll blow you away.'

He kept guns and knives near him because he felt that he wasn't good with his fists. He needed proper protection. He wasn't really thinking. He just followed the older boys and did what they did. That's how he spent the days and nights. Smoking weed and robbing and mugging.

He got into the new drug of choice. It was a craze that appeared on the streets of south London. Crack cocaine. It was the summer of 1995. It was like a storm. Jamaican immigrants started selling vast quantities of the stuff, then everyone was trying to get their hands on it. The word on the streets around Bloods was that everyone wanted to get hold of crack. Angell Town erupted in fights between the 28s and the Untouchables. There were the Portuguese doing their stuff; the Yardies were on the block; the Africans were selling on the block too, and the English were doing their robberies. It was mad and hectic. The drug game was rising and Bloods was in the thick of it. He was hanging out with the Yardie boys and the 28s and causing chaos. He knew that he was trying to forget something. It was a drugged haze of robbery and shotting. And Bloods was doing it all over London.

That's when he was driving around south London with Johnny Peelo, Arch and Drum listening to the Scare Dem Crew and Bounty Killer. That's when they started planning their next robbery as the Peel Dem Crew.

It wasn't long before the police caught up with Bloods. The arrival of crack on the streets had created a backlash and the police were rounding up suspected 'gang bangers' from all over London. Bloods was caught and got sentenced for robbery. He was sent to a young offenders' institution in Dover, but immediately he caused chaos there. He never had any money sent to him in prison so he used to nick things from the other boys or threaten them until they gave him cash. He got sent to the solitary block, but when that didn't work he was quickly moved out to

Feltham and then to the notorious prison on Portland Bill in Dorset. No one wanted to go to Portland. It had the reputation as a hard place. Even Bloods was intimidated. *I don't want to even lie. I was scared to go there.* There were a lot of skinheads and racism was rife. To survive, Bloods went to the gym and built himself up. He made friends with another south London robber and mugger who went by the street name of K Nutz. They were the only black kids on the wing. Ninety per cent of the white guys were racist and the other ten per cent just had to keep quiet. During the first few weeks Bloods was beaten up but after a couple of beatings he began to hold his own.

That's when he received a letter from his old school friend, Elijah Kerr.

Each week he looked forward to JaJa's letters. They sparkled with optimism and hope and plans for the future.

Bloods knew that any day he was going to be put into adult jail and that things would get tougher. He was hyped up. He knew that he was going to have to fight to survive. He was ready to tear the place up. What Bloods wanted most was to be able to share a cell with JaJa. *If JaJa was here we could take on the system.* He remembered how, at school, JaJa was never caught in a fight with anyone but you could see, even then, that you wouldn't want to mess with him. He remembered too how JaJa had come to see him after his mum died. He believed there was a link between them. *I'm superstitious. Everything happens for a reason. I felt him from that time when he came to my house.*

When they finally met up a year later, it would lead to them joining up and turning his four-man band of hoodlums into a gang with real influence on the street.

Chapter Sixteen

The Return of Fat Si

There were the four of us. We were mashing up the roadside. We was making money. We was flying banks. We was steaming money from banks. We was on the road, shotting, selling drugs, buying trainers, mountain bikes, tracksuits. This was when I realized we can make money from weed and crack and heroin. Whatever you could get your hands on, you shott it. It was crazy, man. I loved them times.

Phat Si

It was 1996 when Fat Si got back to England. His grandmother had sent him away from Canada to stop him going to prison. He didn't mind. He was glad to be going back to Angell Town. His dad came to the airport again to pick him up. He noticed the change in atmosphere as soon as he got into Brixton. Angell Town had a different vibe going. Everything was about designer clothes and jewellery: Versace and diamond-encrusted watches. There was a new music on the streets which he hadn't heard in Toronto.

They called it 'Jungle'. And instead of weed and heroin there seemed to be a craze for crack.

Fat Si was no longer fat. His spell in prison, his weed habit, his full-on sex life had made him lean and mean. He was tall anyway, and broad shouldered. But now he was muscly and fit. When he reached Angell Town he went straight round to JaJa's at Marston House. He knocked on the door and his mum answered.

'Elijah's's not here. He's in Feltham.'

'What the hell is Feltham?'

Fat Si had no idea what or where Feltham was. He had no real idea what jail was.

He walked through the estate to the park and found two of the Cole brothers, Skippy and his younger brother Byron, an Asian kid that they'd grown friendly with whose street name was Phong, and the two Cross brothers, Inch and Biker. He was pleased that they were all still there. The older boys had plans. Fat Si was intent on making as much money from drugs as he could.

'We're gonna mash up the roadside.'

They were going to buy up crack cocaine and heroin from the Yardie men and the Turks and Portuguese and sell them off to the 'cats' for a profit. With the money they planned to buy mountain bikes, trainers and tracksuits. Whatever drugs they could lay their hands on they would 'shott'. Shotting was where it was at.

He'd only been back three days when it went wrong.

I'll never forget what happened. I picked up a bag of 'B', a bag of heroin wrapped in cellophane, from this drug den. It was fifty quid's worth. I didn't have to pay for it. I got it. I'd have to pay for it later. That's how it worked. And I was on the Stockwell Park Estate and something told me not to be there. I'm thinking where shall I set up shop? And I turned round and the old Bill was there and they've gone through my pockets and found my wraps and then they searched my gran's house. It was a drama thing. Nothing was there. I said, 'Go on, take me to jail.' There was one motherfucker who was on my arse the whole time. I'll never forget his badge number. 156.

Policeman 156 wouldn't let up.

'You're supplying class A drugs.'

'I've got a habit. I'm not selling the stuff.'

'Come with us.'

They looked at his records but found nothing. They had no idea about the trouble he'd had in Toronto, nor the lengthening criminal record stored on the Canadian police computer system. They gave him a conditional discharge. When he got out of Brixton police station he breathed a sigh of relief. But it didn't stop him. The next day he was on the road again. He carried on shotting with the others.

Chapter Seventeen

Customer Service

To be in with the crowd I had to be in with them. I had to do what they were doing. That's how it works.

Birdie

Birdie had managed to stay out of trouble like he swore he would. He was younger than Fat Si and JaJa, and didn't feel under the same pressure to do what they were doing. When JaJa was sent to Feltham, Birdie reminded himself again that he mustn't get caught. While Fat Si and Inch and the others were smoking weed, Birdie stayed clear of that. Someone had once given him some hash and mixed it with skunk. Skunk was a more potent form of weed. It didn't give him a buzz. It gave him a headache and made him fall asleep at school. So, instead of hanging around and smoking with the others he put his efforts into playing football. He built a team called the Lambeth Tigers, based around young 'gang bangers' and hangers-on, and they would play twice a week, winning tournament after tournament. There was even a match against the police. The Tigers won.

After school Birdie got a place in college. It was a surprise to the school authorities because no one had given him any hope of getting anywhere. But he passed his GCSEs easily.

They were all shocked coz they thought I wasn't working.
But I've always been like that. It may not look like I'm
working but I'm getting it done.

Birdie was good with numbers. He enrolled in an advanced class of business studies at a local college. He found the course easy. He learned how to write a business plan and how to do basic accountancy. The trouble was that he saw his friends on the estate buying Moschino and Versace clothes and £100 trainers while he was still trying to live off pocket-money.

It was too much for him.

He couldn't bear it any longer.

He stopped going to classes and told his mum that he was on a day off. Then he began to hang around again with Inch, Fat Si and Fat Chris and sell drugs. Even though he was only 16 years old he was getting £100 a day.

What Birdie had going for him was that he was sensible and still swore that he would not go to prison. He would meet up with the Yardie men on Brixton Road, get some weed or brown off them and promise to pay it back. Then he would go out and get his clientele. He was good at it. Customers trusted him. He was always nice and treated them well.

It's old fashioned customer service. Everyone likes me.
Everyone would want to go to me rather than other people.
If you cuss your customers and talk bad they won't come

back. But if you treat people well they will come back for more. I had most of Brixton under lock.

He wasn't interested in smoking his own supply. He'd seen it go pear-shaped for several pushers who got hooked on their own gear. They ended up getting beaten up by their own suppliers.

In a few weeks Birdie was making 'ps', for 'paper', 'paper notes'. He was making money. He joined in with Fat Si and the others, but at the same time he kept apart, making sure that he didn't fall into the madness. He stood back and noticed that the younger kids on the estate, kids like the Cole brothers, were already following in the footsteps of the older kids.

Byron Cole was now 10 years old. It didn't take long for him to graduate from solo muggings and shoplifting. His mum gave him nothing to live on so when he saw his brothers and his brothers' friends with new trainers it started up something deep inside him. He was glad therefore when the older boys from the 28s and the Younger 28s recruited him for robbery. Just like JaJa a few years before, he helped the older boys rob houses and 'tief' radios, known as 'pull-outs', from cars. They used to jimmy open windows and, because he was small, Byron would climb in and open the door.

The older boys gave him a street name. 'Mad Dog' was the first name, but then a guy called Smokey looked at him and named him the younger 'Ribz'. He was skinny and looked like one of Smokey's 'bredren', another guy called 'Ribs' who was one of the older boys in the 28s. At first he didn't like the name because he thought they were taking the piss. But soon everyone was calling him 'the younger Ribz' and after a while it grew on him and he just accepted it.

That's how street life is. Having a tag is like gaining more respect. It means I'm something out there. In our little circle everyone has a name when you are up there, innit? It means that when I do tings, certain people don't know who you are, they only know what the streets call you, innit?

With his street name or tag, he felt like someone. He looked at everyone's Nike trainers and realized he didn't have to rely on the big boys.

From about 10 years old I went by myself, like robbing people and that. Crime just got me. It got bigger and bigger until it was like an addiction. When I bought my first pair of trainers myself, that's when it became a problem. That's when I thought I can do this on my own. I don't need no one. My mum gave me nothing anyway. She was going through her own problems. I see my friends with new trainers and that and it used to play on my mind and I thought I know how to get it. So I went out and got it.

That's when he started robbing schools, shops, houses in a big way. He ran riot. His mum didn't notice. He didn't see much of her. When she wasn't out of her head on dope, she was in prison.

Then something happened which would bother Ribz for years to come.

It was in Holloway prison in north London. He'd gone there

to visit his mum who was back inside serving yet more time for drug offences. This time she'd been in about a year. He walked into a large, plain, anonymous room filled with tables and chairs where family and friends were sitting waiting to talk to inmates. The prison officers brought out his mum and they sat down ready to begin an awkward conversation. Ribz looked around. There were about fourteen other people who'd come for visiting hours, each with kids in tow. His mum leaned into him and pointed to some kids who were at the table next door.

'That's your brother and sister over there.'

Ribz couldn't take in what she was saying at first.

'And that woman next to me is the mother of your father's babies.'

Then it began to sink in what she was saying. He glanced over at the two little kids his mum had pointed out.

I was shocked, they were younger and I was thinking, 'How? No way.' I was thinking, 'How's that possible?' I'd never seen them in my life. They never came out of my mum. I didn't want to believe it.

His mum then told him that his father had children with a couple of other women who were now locked up with her in prison. And he probably had lots of children around the estate.

Ribz's eyes opened wider. He felt freaked out.

That's when Ribz realized he had lots of brothers and sisters living around Brixton. But he had no idea who they were.

It changed his life forever. When he got back to Angell Town he looked around at the faces of other boys and girls on the estate and wondered whether any of them were related to him.

Suddenly he felt bad about having a crush on a girl. *I wonder if she is my sister. That's not right to fancy my sister.* The thought of flirting with a girl who might be his half-sister did his head in. It was an anxiety that constantly gnawed at him. It never went away.

After that he always wondered about what had become of the two kids he'd seen in prison. But he never saw them again.

Life began to spiral out of control for Ribz. He was sent to different schools but was thrown out of all of them. First Brockwell School in Tulse Hill, then Allen Edwards in Stockwell. Eventually he was sent to a special school in Tooting called Beechcroft for kids with learning and behavioural difficulties. It took people from all over London. It was the school you were sent to when no other school would accept you. But Ribz felt even more messed up there than anywhere else. He felt he was in prison. He tried to smash windows and run away and cause trouble but the staff just hit him and put him into body locks, the sort of body holds he'd seen on television programmes about mental institutions. It only made Ribz fight even more. But there were only so many beatings he would take. That's when he managed to escape. He ran back to live on the streets of the only place he knew. He ran back to Angell Town. And that's when he saw his 'cousin' get shot in the face, right in front of him. It was outside the Angell Town clubhouse. Ribz was there, Inch was there, Birdie was there, Fat Si was there. And one of them was waving a gun.

Chapter Eighteen

The Shooting

When it's good, street life is exciting. That's why it's dangerous.
JaJa

The shooting took place just days after Fat Si's conditional discharge for drug possession. It was the biggest thing to happen in Angell Town. It wasn't so much that it was a shooting. There had been shootings before. Birdie had seen several Yardie men get shot up outside his home at Pym House when he was growing up. There had also been stabbings and shoot-outs whenever a petty dispute broke out. But this shooting was in the heart of Angell Town, near Marston House, right outside the Angell Town clubhouse. And it was a shooting that had been brewing for some time.

The arguments started off outside a house next to the Angell Town club. One of Angell Town's notorious families lived there. The family had some friends in town. Or maybe they were relatives. No one quite knew. Anyway, they were new to the area and wanted to make a point. But those who had been brought up on the estate knew that you don't mess around with people from Angell Town.

Some weeks earlier Fat Si, Birdie and some of the other Younger 28s were hanging around in someone's garden when the new guys walked past with their tops off, flaunting their muscles.

Fat Si looked up.

The new guys stared back at him provocatively.

'What are you looking at?'

Birdie knew it was the wrong thing to say.

You don't go to someone's area and say, 'What are you looking at?' You don't know what can happen to you. Not in a place like Angell Town.

That's how it started. The new guys thought Fat Si was disrespecting them. But Fat Si was with his mates. It wasn't until they found Fat Si alone that the argument escalated. They beat him up. Outside the chip shop. The word spread that the new guys were trying to make a point to the residents of Angell Town.

It was a Wednesday. It was the middle of the day. It was baking hot. Some people were inside the Angell Town club playing table tennis, others were outside gathering on the street. There were about twenty people there. Ribz was there. Birdie was there. Inch was there. There was no reason to think that things weren't cool.

Suddenly there was shouting and screaming and cussing. Some people got pushed. Someone punched someone. Some people were off their heads. Fat Si had a revolver. Ribz's cousin was in the middle of a mêlée. Someone yelled. Someone pushed someone. It got heated.

Bang. Bang. Bang. Inch ran out of the clubhouse. Bang, bang, bang. Inch was met with a chaotic scene.

Everyone was out there and there were more gunshots. Bang, bang, bang, bang. Young kids crying, everyone was scattering. It was hectic. That was the first big incident around here. Someone had been shot. I didn't know the guy. We were all young. There was blood everywhere, man. He'd been shot in the face.

More shots were fired. Fat Si was waving his revolver. People screamed. People ran. The clubhouse emptied. Inch had never seen anything like it. Birdie saw someone fall to the ground. There was panic. It was hectic. Ribz was standing right there in the middle of it. Lying on the ground was his cousin Elijah Morrisson. There was blood on the pavement. There was blood dripping from his head. Fat Si ran off still waving the revolver.

The ambulance came. The police came. But no one really talked.

Fat Si's friends gathered round him.

'You've got to breeze. They will say it's you. First things first. It's no good going back to Angell Town.'

Fat Si didn't have any money. He was constantly broke. All the money he'd got from robbing and shotting he'd 'spunked' on trainers, tracksuits, alcohol and raves. He went round first to his dad's, then to his grandma's, and said that he needed money. He didn't tell them why.

Sharon Kerr, JaJa's mum, was pleased that her son was still in jail and wasn't there for the shooting. It was bound to happen. Rivalries between the different groups always ended up in shootings or stabbings. She was used to seeing them on her doorstep. And the police could do nothing about it.

*Police were more scared back in the old days, because it was
more enclosed. Back in the old days they couldn't control
what went on. They were scared to come in. There were so
many places to hide that they didn't like coming in here.*

It was to do with the way the estate was built. Although, in some
ways, Sharon thought it was like a prison, anyone fleeing from the
police could get away by 'jumping the block'. It meant jumping
over the wall separating one block from another. Because Marston
House, Ireton House and Pym House were all joined by the pedways, Sharon knew how easy it was to find an escape route.

*You couldn't find anybody in Angell Town. You could do
things there and get away with it. Only the people in Angell
Town knew where everybody was because most of us knew
the estate like the back of our hand. If you put a child in a
playpen it will make use of what it's got there, naturally.*

And that's how Fat Si got away from the police. He ran through
the back alleys of the estate, got hold of some money and within
days he was on a flight to Canada. He needed to get away. He
wanted to get away. It was as though he could never be satisfied in
one place. It was as though he always had to run. Wherever he
went he seemed to attract trouble. Just three months after his
arrival in London, he was once again back on a plane to Toronto.
His sister picked him up from the airport and took him home. He
dropped off his bags, handed out money and presents to his mum
and sisters and went straight round to see his girlfriend Lisa.

She was waiting for him. She looked different. She had news
for him. She was pregnant. Pregnant by him. She told him that

she had got pregnant just before he'd left Canada for England when he was still 15. She hadn't told him. She hadn't told her parents. She didn't want them to know because she didn't want to be forced to have an abortion. She was skinny and small so she managed to hide her pregnancy by wearing big clothes. When she finally did tell her parents they were pleased for her.

Fat Si too was pleased.

I've got a baby on the way. I'm going to get my life together and be more mature. I plan to get serious. I did mature. I was growing up.

He was 16 years old. He started to pay rent to live at his sister's rather than living at his mum's for free. He'd arrived just in time. Within days of his arrival from London he was in a Toronto hospital watching his girlfriend give birth.

It changed my life. I've never seen nothing like that, seeing that baby come out. The way the head came out of the vagina, then popped back in again then popped out again. A whole head of hair and I nearly fainted, man. But it was the most gorgeous thing I'd ever seen. I was young. I was only 16.

Fat Si helped cut the umbilical cord. It was a boy.

Chapter Nineteen

Inch and Ribz

I was sick of wearing black pumps to school, just because they're gonna last long. No. I wanted the latest Adidas or Air Max trainers.

Inch

A ngell Town was in shock after the shooting. The only good news was that although the bullet had penetrated the skull, the victim, Elijah Morrisson, hadn't died. The bullet had passed within an inch of the brain but was now so deeply embedded in the victim's head that surgeons thought it safer to leave it there. What was most shocking was that the shooting had happened in broad daylight, outside the clubhouse which was at the very centre of the planned Angell Town regeneration project. Parents were jumpy. They kept the younger children close to them. The older kids too were shocked by what they had seen. As the police looked for suspects, life in Angell Town calmed down. For a while anyway.

* * *

Inch had never got into trouble even though he had been observing JaJa's criminal activities from afar. He'd seen the good things robbery could bring. He also saw the bad things. When JaJa had got his three-year sentence, Inch had been shocked.

It was unthinkable. What the fuck? The judge gave him three years. Properly three years. That was unknown. He was a couple of years older than me. How could he get three years? I'd never heard of it before.

But even though JaJa was now in prison it hadn't lessened what Inch now began to see as the glamour of a life of robbing and shotting. Seeing everyone else with new, fashionable clothes was too much for Inch.

On the street you needed to look good to get any sort of respect. You needed smart clothes and nice jewellery. He started to follow in JaJa's footsteps and organize his own petty robberies. Housebreaking, steaming, handbag-snatching. With the money he bought nice trainers and Versace clothes. And that's when his relationship with his parents began to break down.

My parents must have known because they saw me in Versace designer wear. They must have known. There was nothing I wanted that they could give me.

There were arguments at home. His dad was mad with him. He saw the 'cats', the punters, queuing up outside the block for drugs and he saw Inch rushing in and rushing out. He put two and two together.

'If you're gonna do it, go and do it elsewhere. I've been

through things in my time. This is my house. If you want to be out late at night then you can't live here. This drug-selling is madness.'

Inch didn't have much of an answer.

'I'm gonna go live somewhere else then.'

It was only much later that he understood what his dad was trying to do.

It's like a cycle, innit? He was trying to keep me on the straight and narrow. Obviously he's seen things in his time and they know that people before them went through the same thing and people before them went through the same thing. D'you get me? And as his kids grow up they're gonna go through the same thing and see the same thing. My dad used to smoke and be a soundman for a band and so he knows about it. He's not dumb to the world and he has been there himself. Not to that extent that we are, though. My older brother was a bit smarter and doing it on the quiet.

Inch was 15. He wanted to go and do his own stuff. He decided to leave Angell Town. Even though he was not the oldest in the family he was the first to leave the family home at Pym House. He got a place in a hostel in Lewisham and paid the rent by signing on. Every week he went to the local post office to get his cheque so he could pay the rent. He enjoyed being free. He knew it was the right time to leave Angell Town and his parents. He needed to get his stuff together. At the same time he found it difficult to cope on Sundays. He missed the Sunday lunches when the whole family would gather round and eat together. But he had cousins in Lewisham and hung out with them there.

He had a moped and sometimes he'd go back to Angell Town. Even though JaJa was in prison and Fat Si had gone to Canada, there were still people who he could hang with. Fat Chris, Skippy, Kojo and Ribz. Because they were on the road, robbing and shotting, they all had money. One of the older boys, either Fat Wayne or Kelvin, would 'get a rental' from a local car rental company and they would all pile in and go to the West End. It was a chilled-out time. They had money and they were cool. And Inch managed to stay out of trouble.

Ribz didn't have it so good. Inch was careful. He made sure he was never caught. Ribz, though, didn't seem to care whether he was caught or not. He was 15 when his house got 'kicked off' by the police. At first Ribz thought they were after one of his older brothers. They were the ones who were always getting into trouble and going to jail. He turned to his brother.

'You're in trouble. What have you done?'

He was kind of shocked therefore when the police turned to him.

'We don't want him. We've come for you.'

Ribz was charged with thirty-two burglaries in the area. They had his fingerprints at all thirty-two scenes. He was too young for prison so he was sent to secure units all over the country. He caused problems wherever he went. He never settled in. He avoided making himself comfortable on purpose. He knew that wherever they sent him would never be his home.

I never tried because I never felt 100 per cent comfortable.
No matter what they tried to buy me, how much they tried
to make me settle, I used to do my own thing coz I knew
they didn't care a fuck about me.

He began the rounds of secure units first in Liverpool, then Camberwell, then all over the country. But none of them could control him. He smashed windows and fought and hit the staff.

At one children's unit outside London he nearly burnt the place down. Trouble had been brewing for some time. Two of the male staff there used to piss Ribz off. He thought they were perverts. One was a white guy, the other an Asian. They were only young, in their early twenties, but Ribz thought they were 'moving' to the young girls. Out of the corner of his eye he saw them touching up the young girls and flirting with them. Ribz's resentment grew. He and a mate of his, Kermit, who'd been at school with him in south London, used to 'brush' the two male staff members, by bumping into them in the corridors and giving them dirty looks and muttering 'perv' as they walked by. But Ribz also resented the girls. He thought some of the girls were mad, acting all sexual and enjoying the sexual games. It exploded one afternoon when the oldest girl, who was about 16, stepped out of the bathroom with a robe around her. She shouted over to Ribz.

'Come, come, come over here.'

Ribz walked over to her.

She dropped her robe and opened her legs. Blood started dripping down her leg.

'What the hell...?'

Ribz was still only a young kid and although he knew something was up he didn't really understand about a girl's period. He didn't understand why blood was coming out from between her legs.

He felt squeamish. He felt disturbed and humiliated. He felt horrified.

That night he crawled into her dormitory while she was sleeping and slithered under her bed. With a knife he slashed the mattress and began pulling out some of the straw filling. Then he took a lighter and set fire to the mattress's innards.

The mattress caught light immediately, sending flames up to the ceiling. Luckily everyone, including the girl, managed to get out. The fire brigade was called but the staff managed to put the fire out with fire extinguishers before it spread. Ribz got into some serious trouble for it. Fortunately though the police never took it further. The girl covered for him and said it was an accident.

It wasn't until he was sent to a secure unit in Stratford in east London that he felt kind of comfortable and calmed down. The place doubled as a detention centre for illegal immigrants and he was there with a group of Kosovans who were waiting to be deported. It was the first time that he'd ever met anyone who spoke such a different language but it didn't stop him from getting on with them. He used to see them the whole time in the facility's dining room. Nobody was allowed to eat anywhere other than in the dining room, so whenever Ribz came down he would be faced with the group of Kosovans tucking into a large feast of meat kebabs and melted cheeses. While Ribz made himself his usual cheese sandwich they would babble to him with a smile on their faces and mouths full of spicy sausage. They always gave him some of their food. He thought they were all cool guys. The best part of being in Stratford though was that if he left early enough in the morning he could take the bus, get to Angell Town and hang out with his brothers and some of the gang for a few hours before heading back to east London for curfew.

When he turned 16 the routine of travelling between various secure units and foster homes changed. He was back in court for a long list of offences that he'd committed a year earlier. He was sentenced to twelve months. This time he was sent to Feltham. He was excited. He'd always wanted to go to prison. He was so happy that he danced a jig in the prison van.

> *It was kinda exciting for me still, the first time. I really wanted to go to jail. Everyone used to boast about it, innit? It was like a craze. I remember saying to myself, 'I wanna go to jail, I wanna go to jail.' So when I did go I was kinda excited. I'd never been in a prison van and going to Feltham I was so excited still that I was all like dancing and everything. When I got there that's when it hit me that my freedom was being took away.*

What made it OK was that both of his brothers were there. Both of them. And several guys that he knew from Angell Town. He knew he'd get through it. *This is OK. I don't care. This isn't too bad.*

With JaJa in prison, Fat Si in Canada and Ribz in various foster homes and detention centres around the UK, Inch slowly expanded his stomping ground outside the narrow boundaries of Angell Town and south London. He had a cousin called Adrian who lived in Lewisham. Adrian had a mate, a big, scary black bloke who had got mixed up with Triad gangs in Chinatown in London's West End. The Triad gangsters had hired the friend as 'muscle'. His job was to get a crew together and go and scare restaurant owners and shopkeepers in Chinatown into paying up protection money. If the restaurant owner paid up the crew would promise to protect him from rival gangs. If they didn't pay up there would be trouble. Inch soon became part of the crew. It started off as 'dumb stuff', running around scaring people, just intimidating them. But sometimes it went further. The crew would corner a scared shopkeeper in Chinatown's Gerrard Street and take out 'choppers' or knives and threaten to 'run him down' unless he paid up. Sometimes full-blown turf wars would break out with rival Triad gangs and their crews. And Inch was in the thick of it. He knew what was going on. It was pure racketeering but he enjoyed being involved. In Chinatown he began to get a reputation as a 'mad black brother'.

Chapter Twenty

Hats, Nikes and Guns

When I come out everything had changed. Guns was
out more, drugs was out more. Everything was more out in
the open. Music was more out in the open, guns was more
out in the open, drugs was more out in the open.

JaJa

As Ribz went into Feltham, JaJa came out. It was the summer of 1998, and for JaJa everything was different. First he noticed how tall his little brother was. JaJa had only been gone eighteen months but Naja was now taller than him. Some of the younger guys like Inch and Birdie had also grown bigger. They were real grown-ups now. There were new people on the block too and the flat in Marston House looked different, smaller somehow. Bling-bling jewellery and Versace clothes were everywhere. At night he noticed that guns were visible on the street. Most of his friends now carried a 'stick', stuffed into their waistbands.

It was partly a fashion statement, partly a power thing.
Hats, Nikes and guns. That's what got respect on the streets.

He was surprised to see that more people were dealing drugs out in the open. And the music was more in your face. There was D 'n' B fever, drum 'n' bass. Cars were no longer pumping out the fast Jungle music. It was now slower, deeper, thumping beats that bounced off the walls of the blocks at Pym House, Marston House and Ireton House and made the air vibrate around Angell Town.

While he was in prison, JaJa had practised his rapping. Sometimes he was pleased with it. He rapped because it made sense of the life he was leading. He could tell it like it was and often the bars or short lines of lyrics came out well, as good as the American rap artists like Snoop Dog that he used to listen to. Other times it came out wrong and he got frustrated at how bad it sounded. It was important for him to get it right. His rapping was all part of his plan to get his music business going.

He started promoting music events, and putting together raves, just like he'd promised to do while he was in prison.

One evening, as he was coming out of a music event he noticed two cars pull up slowly outside the venue. The car windows lowered and the barrels of two Mac 10s, military issue submachine guns, appeared out of the darkness inside. He knew what was going to happen. He ducked.

Vrooomm. Vrooomm.

People started screaming and dived to the ground. The cars drove off. He wasn't hit and he couldn't tell if anyone else was hit but there was glass all over the place. He didn't think they were aiming at him but how could he tell? He knew Angell Town and Brixton well enough to know that feuds could go back a long way.

Feuds could be over something important like revenge for a murder, or something stupid like the wrong sort of look. He wasn't scared and he didn't try to think about it too much. The aims and motives of a drive-by shooting were too complicated to sort out. He wasn't that bothered by it.

It takes more than that to get us scared. Probably because of all the things we've been through. I've been through loads of things. I'd be more scared if something happened to one of my friends or one of my bredren, d'you know what I'm saying? Like if I hear that Naja has gone somewhere and there'd been a shooting, straightaway that would scare me. It's more love that gets me scared. Losing someone close to me.

Bloods had come out a couple of months before JaJa. He didn't hang around. He went straight out to the block in Stockwell and started hustling and shotting. Prison hadn't reformed him. He'd never even thought about reforming. He got out of prison and went straight back into a life of crime. He tried to stay away from guns, though. He'd got into guns before he went to prison and he knew they meant trouble.

If anything could keep him indoors it was music. In his front room in Stockwell, he and his friend Arch started making music. At first it was reggae bars, then drum 'n' base, then a new sound.

Hip-hop. Now I'm feeling hip-hop.

It wasn't the old school hip-hop he was into. He was into hard-core hip-hop.

His friend Quinney, a guy he had known from the streets and from prison, joined in. With a stereo in the front room they started rapping. One day Quinney came out with a bar.

'I've got an angel on one side and a demon on the other.'

For Quinney the rap was personal. One side was telling him to be good. The other side was telling him to be bad. In Quinney's case, the demon was telling him to kill his 'brudder', someone who had always disrespected him.

But it meant something for Bloods too. It was what he always felt, the conflict between doing good and doing bad. He would never forget that line about the devil and the angel.

'Fuck. I wanna rap.'

That's what he told anyone who would listen.

And that's what he told JaJa.

JaJa and Birdie went round to Bloods's place in Stockwell. They wanted to renew the friendship they'd started in prison. They started talking about taking music seriously. They needed a name for their crew. Bloods suggested the Peel Dem Crew or Pil Dem Crew, the name that he had come up with when he was doing his 'stick-ups' in south London. JaJa liked it. He now recognized the initials 'PDC' from the letters he and Bloods had exchanged in prison. It's how Bloods always signed off his letters. PDC. It was a good name. JaJa was just out of prison. He had a name on the estate. Everyone knew him and he knew everyone.

Soon the name 'PDC' had spread. Soon everyone on the estate was talking about the PDC. Everyone wanted to join in.

JaJa had PDC tattooed on his neck so that everyone could

see. The name went out to those in Angell Town, Kennington, Stockwell, as well as to those in prison. There was Bloods and Quinney and K Nutz and all those, like Inch and Ribz, who were in the Younger 28s. It was JaJa who linked everyone. It was JaJa who brought them all together into the new crew.

> *The drug game bonded people around us. All of us from Angell Town, we were bonding. That's how it became like a big family, a big unit, and during this time it gets bigger and people are talking about the Peel Dem Crew. There was lots of shootings and lots of talk about selling drugs on the block with the Peel Dem Crew. Shootings and robbings and drugging. We were on the street doing our thing. That's how the PDC started as a gang.*

They tried to make some money out of the rapping but their attempts were unfocused. Inspired by Bloods, JaJa redoubled his rapping efforts. He managed to rent a studio and started putting down some tunes. But it was tough. JaJa had hoped that the music promotion and raves would get them rich and make them famous. But the money didn't come in. Things got hard again. He wanted clothes and trainers. *I need more money so I need to up my game*. He didn't want to rob so he started selling drugs again. He bought quantities of drugs at wholesale prices and cut them into smaller quantities and sold them in Angell Town.

That's when he first began to understand how the drug game really worked.

If he wanted small quantities of drugs he could get them

from the Portuguese or the Yardies round the corner. But if he wanted large quantities of drugs, he had to leave the estate and go to richer areas. And that's when he got a surprise.

He contacted a mate of his.

'I need weed. Lots of it.'

'I know someone. I'll introduce you.'

They got in a car and left Brixton and headed out to south-east London, where the houses got bigger and the streets leafier. They stopped in a tree-lined avenue in a well-to-do neighbour-hood. JaJa had never been there before but the houses were much bigger than those round Brixton. They sat in the car and waited. JaJa expected a black bloke to come ambling along at any moment and tap on the window. Instead, through the rear mirror he saw an oldish-looking white man walking along the road towards them. JaJa was worried.

I was thinking there were too many proper big houses and nice people and we shouldn't stay in this road too long. If people like that see us they'll see two black guys in the car on a road like this and call the police.

The old man started coming towards them.

JaJa turned to his mate, concerned.

'Who's this?'

'That's our man.'

'What? You must be joking.'

The two of them got out of the car and went with the man to one of the big houses set back from the road. JaJa expected that at any moment someone else would come along, his son or someone, and take over the negotiations. It didn't happen. The man walked right up a gravel driveway into the large house and took them through a nice hallway and carpeted sitting room where a woman who must have been his wife was watching *EastEnders* and tucking into tea and biscuits. Two kids were playing with a dog nearby. None of them seemed to think it at all strange that two black blokes were walking through the middle of their nice sitting room.

They walked through into a conservatory where pots of weed were growing everywhere. JaJa couldn't believe his eyes as he stepped into what looked like a proper cannabis factory at the back of the house.

There was a big machine that was spinning some sort of material.

'What's that?'

'That's piss. It helps fertilize the dirt and reacts with the alkaloids in the plant. It makes the skunk more potent.'

JaJa was disgusted. He didn't realize that when he smoked skunk he was breathing in urine. From then on he made a vow never to smoke the stuff again. And he never did.

They paid about £5,000 and took away two carrier bags of weed. Just before they left the old white guy told them to wait. He got on the mobile phone and talked to someone in a low voice.

JaJa and his mate went back down the drive and got into their car. When they drove off a car appeared from nowhere and immediately sat on their tail. His mate explained that it was for security. If the police tried to stop them the car behind would ram the cop car, allowing them to get away. That's how organized the old man's operation was.

JaJa was impressed. So impressed that he immediately started to hatch a plan to go back there and rob the place.

'So, who was that guy?'

'He's the boss man. The man in charge.'

JaJa's mate told him that the only reason they had met the white guy was because his usual contact, a Yardie man who was the middleman between the white guy and the punters in south London, was doing some business in Jamaica.

It was information that opened JaJa's eyes. After that he understood the economics of the operation better. The white guy sold bags of weed to the Yardie who had a network of black guys, like franchisees, who would sell the stuff over south London to smaller guys working on the street like JaJa. The white man would sell the carrier bag full of weed for £2,500 and as it went down the chain each person would take their cut until the same carrier bag, minus a few ounces that had been creamed off as 'handling charges', would get down to JaJa's level. JaJa might be able to make a profit of a couple of hundred quid by breaking the weed down to smaller amounts of an ounce or nine ounces, called a 'nine bar', and selling it on to guys even lower down the chain. They, in their turn, would sell it on to someone else. There was always someone starting out in the game who was prepared to make a few quid for their own little hustle.

JaJa calculated that the white guy was making thousands of pounds each transaction. That's how he could afford to sit there chilling in front of the telly while JaJa roamed the streets.

A few weeks later when he'd finished his stash, JaJa went back to the leafy suburb and tried to get some more skunk. The white guy, though, just stood on his doorstep and told him that it was all finished.

I think the guy read my thoughts about wanting to rob the

place. He must have had a funny feeling coz he wouldn't
sell any more to me after that.

A couple of years later, when JaJa was in prison, he saw on the news that there had been a raid on a cannabis factory in south London. The pictures showed the same house he had been to two years earlier. The news reporter said that nine people had been arrested. But when the photos of the suspects came up on the telly they were of two black Yardie men looking mean and nasty and greedy. They didn't show the 'Grandad' or any white guys. JaJa couldn't help but laugh.

This game is proper fucked up. I reckon the black guys got
more time. They probably found stolen mobile phones and
drugs on them while the white guy got off because he was
old and had arthritis. The black guys probably got seven
years in Belmarsh. That's how the drug game goes.

It was all a revelation to JaJa. He began to realize that the Yardies or the black players weren't in control of the trade. It was always a white man.

The white lads do everything. They do Es and drugs and
they do everything, know what I'm saying. They got
everything, club nights, shops, guns. They got their dads
and uncles in big places, they might have an uncle who is
an MP, know what I'm saying. If I'm selling drugs, back in
the days everyone I meet, the top man, the biggest weed
players and weed dens they were normal white guys living
in posh areas whose kids go to posh schools.

He didn't think too much of it at the time, but somewhere in his brain the knowledge that he was only a small player in a much bigger game began to take root. It was a resentment that would grow. But for the moment there was too much money to be made. He stopped thinking and started shotting. Whatever JaJa could get hold of he sold. Weed, crack, heroin. He had the estate 'on lockdown'.

It was a hectic end to the summer. There were shootings and robberies as the PDC pushed out other dealers. The Yardies got pushed out. The Portuguese got sidelined. And in the middle of it all, everyone was talking about the PDC.

And there were girls. JaJa knew that the girls got off on the excitement he created around himself. Girls were bored and frustrated being at home with their mothers, being got at the whole time, being told what to do. He understood his power over them. He understood that if he created enough glamour around himself they would flock to him. He had money to take them to the cinema and money to take them out of the estate. People recognized him and respected him. The girls got caught up in the same excitement. That's how he fended off the boredom. Music, money, excitement and girls.

Chantelle, JaJa's sister, noticed it too. All her friends pestered her about JaJa.

'Chantelle, your brother is really good.'

Chantelle knew that he had a name on the estate. And she knew how attractive that was for the girls in Angell Town.

Any boy that's got a name you are bound to get stalked by girls. Even if you are not interested. Even if you are trying

146

not to have a girlfriend you don't have a choice, the girl will approach you.

'Chantelle, your brother is really popular. Will you put in a word with him? I want to be with him.'

Sometimes the approach was more direct and they would go up to him directly, especially when the rapping started. When he was doing his rapping the girls would go mad for him.

Chantelle, though, didn't go mad for the other boys. She had a baby on the way. She was 15.

If you have a baby it calms you down. I got calmed down.

Chapter Twenty-one

Inch Does Time

*It was fun. A scary type of fun. It was fun but not fun.
There were people I knew in there from Angell Town but it
was strange going into a place like that, somewhere I'd
never been before. It was going to be mad, but fuck it.*

Inch

The younger boys like Inch had always looked up to JaJa.
But when he came out of prison, they gave him even more
respect. For Inch it was as though he had acquired more experience, as though he was a bigger, better person, someone to look
up to. And he was full of energy. JaJa would always think of
ways to make money. He was moving.

Inch was 16. He'd never been in trouble. He'd begun to rob
and deal drugs and 'roll' with some of his mates who had got
themselves a reputation as 'muscle' for Triad racketeering gangs,
but he'd never been caught. Then it started to go wrong. He was
at home one day when the police barged in and grabbed him.
They can't be after me. It must be a mistake. He had the impression

148

that they didn't know what they were doing, that they didn't know who they were grabbing.

They tried to pin his arms behind his back but Inch was fit and squat and he put up a struggle.

'Get off me. I didn't do nufin'.'

Inch twisted and turned, launching the cops who were trying to handcuff him against the walls and doors of the flat. One of the policemen let out a yelp.

'You've injured me. We are going to do you for assault.'

They got him down to the police station and they charged him. But it was his first offence and he was put on remand.

The arrest didn't stop Inch. He was part of the PDC and he took to the road with the rest of them. They steamed building societies and newsagents. Life on the road was hectic. It was mad.

And then he went too far. He travelled with some others from the PDC to Wimbledon. Someone wanted to steal from the bureau de change at the local Lunn Poly travel agents. He knew he didn't need to do it. He had money so it wasn't as though he was desperate. But his friends wanted him to do it. And he was in the PDC now. He had to join in.

They found the Lunn Poly agency and got access to the back room. There was a man inside and they made him open the door. They yelled and hollered and threatened him until he opened the safe. The seconds ticked by. The safe was on a timer and wouldn't open immediately. While they were waiting they didn't realize that one member of the staff had managed to escape and alert the police. When the wail of police sirens reached them, Inch took off, running through the streets of Wimbledon chased by the police. It was just like the movies, except that Inch didn't get away. He ran down side streets looking for his car, but he couldn't remember where he'd left it. The police caught up with him. He was exhausted. As he was arrested he cursed himself. He hadn't needed the money. *I'm stupid. I'm mad. I'm greedy. The worst thing is that we didn't get no money.*

He was sent to Feltham. He got four years. As soon as the prison gates shut behind him he experienced a wave of mixed feelings. He wanted to talk tough like all the PDC who had been there before him but he struggled. He missed doing those things he normally did at home. He missed his mum. He missed his family. He tried to make the best of it, playing table tennis and having a laugh with his friends, but when he was alone he sat in his cell stressing about how long he still had to go.

> *Four years. It's unthinkable. I thought, shit. I'm fucked. Shit, shit. I didn't think I'd get that long. I've never had a proper sentence before. At the same time I knew what I had done. I tried to take other people's money and was going to jail for it. I couldn't cry about it.*

He was moved from Feltham after he stole a rug from the canteen. He didn't know that you were supposed to sign out equipment from the kitchens. He was with Jacob, a friend of his from Angell Town. They thought the rug would look good on the floor of his cell, so Inch just took it. The prison officers found him out and told him he'd be moved to Dover. The place had a bad reputation.

'Watch it. You'll have a bad time down there.'

Inch thought that they were just trying to scare him.

But they weren't joking. He was moved to Dover. There

were six to a cell and he was miserable. Whenever Inch asked the other boys how long they were in for they would say six months or eight months. *A total of six months. That's unthinkable right there.* Inch had already been in jail for six months and still had nearly two years to serve. The length of the sentence got to him. He found himself getting more frustrated and madder. He fought everybody in his cells. He didn't like people. He wanted to fuck them up. He was mad at everybody. *These people are going home and I have to stay.* It was worse because of his short stature. He was squat and people took advantage. *I think I've got short man syndrome.* He got beaten over the head by people picking on him. But in return he gave out several broken noses.

Then he was moved to Aylesbury, and after that Portland. It was a grim, windswept place, situated on an island in the southwest of England. Inside too it was hellish. From the moment he got there Inch was bullied by the prison officers and the white prisoners. They were pretty much all white. It wasn't physical intimidation. It was more verbal. The skinheads made racist remarks and tried to unsettle him with comments and subtle threats.

'Where do you think you are off to, little man?'

'You can't go in the shower.'

'What do you think you are doing?'

The comments and demands and questions went on for months. Inch wanted to fight them but he tried to bite his tongue. There were too many of them to take on. He didn't get many visits because Portland prison was so far away. How could he get his mum to visit an island, in Dorset, in the far south-west of England? They told him that the only way for visitors to get there was to leave home the day before, spend the night at the hostel down the road and visit the next morning before going home again. There was no way he could ask his mum to do that. He'd put her through too much already. She was mad at him. He was the first of her kids to be in prison.

Portland was misery for Inch. But it would get worse for him before it got better.

Chapter Twenty-two

Wanted

I turned 18 years old and I was in solitary confinement in prison in Canada. I was in a strip cell, naked, no windows, no sink, just walls and concrete. I was shitting there, pissing there, sleeping there. I never got no phone calls. No one knew where I was or nufin'. That was the worst moment of my life.

Phat Si

Fat Si was in Toronto and feeling good. He'd got away from Angell Town a couple of days after the guy had been shot outside the clubhouse and now the police in England wouldn't be able to pull him in for questioning. He had a car, he had money coming in and he had his woman and his baby boy. It was 1998 and he was 17. But the good feeling was about to end.

Many of his friends and cousins, like Kelvin and Conrad, had been nicked for selling drugs. Fat Si had so far escaped. But one evening he was in a neighbourhood of Toronto called Willow Ridge. He was selling cocaine. What he didn't realize was that

the police had surveillance cameras trained on his dealing spot.
The exact spot. He was caught bang to rights.

'What's your name?'

'Simon Maitland.'

The officer tapped the name into the computer. Fat Si
noticed a change in the atmosphere, as though an electric shock
had passed through the place.

The police officer in charge spoke up.

'You'd better be serious here because if you have given a fake
name then this is going to get heavy.'

Fat Si didn't know what he was talking about. He didn't
understand why the atmosphere had changed. He hadn't given
a fake name, he'd given his real name.

'Are you sure that's your name?'

Fat Si didn't know what to think. Something was going on.

'OK then. Tyrone Johnson.'

The fake name seemed to get a better response. The computer screen was blank. Fat Si relaxed and kicked back in the
police station waiting to be processed.

On the other side of town, Fat Si's little sister heard rumours that
he had been arrested. She went straight over to the police station. When she arrived at the police counter, she asked for her
brother.

'I've come to see Simon Maitland.'

They checked on the computer.

'We don't have a Simon Maitland here.'

She knew he was there somewhere so she ran back home,
picked up Fat Si's passport and brought it back to the police

station. She showed it to one of the officers in charge. Next thing Fat Si knew was that an officer stormed into the holding cell.

'Your name's not Tyrone Johnson, you little shit. You black bastard. Do you know Interpol have a file on you? Do you know what the English police say about you? You are wanted for attempted murder in London. A shooting.'

Suddenly the world came down on Fat Si.

'What are you talking about?'

'Someone got shot in London, England, and they say you did it.'

He still wasn't sure what it all meant. He was sent to court but they only sentenced him for the drug bust. There was no mention of a shooting. The Interpol file seemed to have been forgotten. He was sent from jail to jail in Canada to serve out a two-year sentence. And he wasn't happy.

He fought, he rebelled, he smashed things up. He spent his eighteenth birthday stripped naked in a cold, bare cell. His head was so full of emptiness that he didn't even wonder what had become of him.

He served his two years and got put on a plane back to England. He thought he was going home. He thought he was going back to Angell Town.

He arrived back at Heathrow Airport in 1999. As he stepped off the plane, CID and immigration officials were waiting for him.

Chapter Twenty-three

Angell Delight

From somewhere to be ashamed of to somewhere to be proud to live in ... the new Angell Town, once a byword for inner city despair.

Lambeth local press, 13 August 1999

JaJa had been out of prison for a year. In Angell Town he had made sure the Peel Dem Crew was growing and evolving. PDC graffiti appeared on the walls of the estate. It was a way of marking territory. The message was sent out to the prisons. It was the first time that JaJa felt he belonged to something.

Throughout the early half of 1999, the PDC controlled the estate. The 28s had got older and had long moved on. Now it was the PDC who had taken over the area, selling heroin, crack and weed from the stairwell of Marston block. Everyone would help out. Some mothers and neighbours would even shout out to warn them when the police were coming.

JaJa didn't feel bad. He was earning a living. He wasn't causing anyone any harm. He looked after the younger kids on the estate and made sure they were OK. It was true that some of the younger guys like Ribz and Inch had been nicked. But JaJa was out and he made a vow. *I'm never going back to prison.*

He was free and back in the familiar world he knew so well.

Beyond the streets surrounding Marston House, though, Angell Town was changing. Not that JaJa saw it. Or rather he saw the posters and the flyers announcing the residents' meetings, the pilot schemes and the architects' plans. He heard the neighbours talking about the regeneration of the area. But he didn't pay much attention. *I don't give a fuck about the arguments over housing.* He just carried on with his thing, the thieving and the shotting.

It came as a surprise therefore when, on 23 April 1999, bull-dozers arrived in the estate and began to demolish Pym House, the concrete council block where Inch and Ribz had grown up. The dark and grotty garages under Ireton House and Marston House where the drug dealers and muggers used to hang out were now cleaned out and were thriving as small workshops and local stores. Dora Boatemah, the resident who had got the pilot scheme up and running to regenerate the area, was still on the warpath. Her local residents' campaign was paying off. She had managed to convince the Department of the Environment and the local authorities to redevelop the estate. A few months after the demolition of Pym House builders moved in to begin a £69 million regeneration of Angell Town. A steel statue of an angel, mounted on a shining marble plinth, went up in the heart of the estate. The headlines in the local newspapers were cau-tiously upbeat: 'Will £60m cause Angell delight?'

When Ribz came out after his six months in Feltham he had nowhere to live. Pym House was being demolished, his mum wasn't around and he didn't want to live with his nan. It was OK though. When he got back to Angell Town his friends gave him a big welcome. From then on he just lived on the streets, going from one friend's house to the next. He stayed with Ashley, sometimes at JaJa's, sometimes back at his old foster home. He didn't see his mum. She was busy doing her own thing and he was busy doing his. He wouldn't see her again until several years later.

He was relieved in a way that he didn't see her. Years of being moved around from place to place meant that he had no bond with his mum anyway.

At the end of the day she's my mum so I love her but also because of the time we never spent with each other, we're kind of distant, do you get me? All my family is distant. We are not as close as we should be. We don't tell each other everything. I'm not going to lie, as I was growing up, once I realized she wasn't around, I didn't really want to be around her, even though I could. The streets was my home. I was so used to being with other people that I didn't want to be around her.

He was glad to be back in Angell Town but he still suffered from the anxiety that he had unknown sisters all over the estate and couldn't really afford to hook up with a girl, just in case.

He suffered real heartache over it. There was a girl he really liked. Her name was Bianca and they'd met one Saturday night at the Fridge nightclub in Brixton. It was where he used to go to chill with his friends. She was from Somerleyton, an estate to the south of Angell Town, just the other side of Brixton's Coldharbour Lane. He really liked her. Once she took him back to meet her family. The girl's mum looked Ribz up and down. He thought she was looking at him oddly.

'I think I know your people.'

Ribz's blood ran cold. He looked at Bianca and strange thoughts started rushing round his head. *Maybe she looks like me. Yes, she does look like me. Maybe she's my sister. Maybe...*

He tried not to think too hard but his relationship with Bianca was never the same after that. Years later he found out that she wasn't related but the damage was done. He would look at everyone, even boys, and wonder whether they were his brothers. It ate away at him, not knowing who his brothers and sisters were. He knew then that he would never feel at ease until he'd tracked down his father to find out who exactly his own flesh and blood were.

Life on the streets stayed hectic for him. He couldn't stay out of trouble. Sometimes it was serious. He went to a club in Camberwell with a couple of his boys. They had guns with them. He knew it was stupid. But that's how it was. The gun thing just happened. An argument started with rivals.

It kinda popped off. One guy tried to move to one of my friends. It was kinda tit for tat. Guns came out and then shooting, shooting, shooting. Someone got hit.

Ribz fired into the crowd. He didn't know whether he'd shot someone or not. It all happened so fast. He didn't really care.

That's what you have to do when you are in the wars. I've been through so much different things. I've been through a lot. Trust me. Seeing my mum go through what she's gone through. Seeing my brothers go through what they've gone through. You have to do it.

Over the next two years Ribz was in and out of court and in and out of prison. He never seemed to be able to stop himself from robbing. As soon as he was out of prison and back on the streets of Angell Town he'd get into difficulty and get put away again. It was always a painful process for him. Unlike some of the others who seemed to be laid back about the cycle of being nicked, spending the night in a police cell, going to court and being sentenced, Ribz had never got used to it. He'd experienced a strange elation the first time he was sent to Feltham, but now, each time he was taken to the police station he used to burst into tears. He was getting so tired of the pattern and found his situation so hopeless that he used to cry his eyes out in the police station cell.

The officer who took down the details never made it any easier for him.

'Back again, mate. What's it for this time?'

Ribz got the impression that they were happy to see him back and on his way to prison. He guessed the police saw it as a result, that they were doing a good job by taking him off the streets.

Arrest, police station, court, prison, arrest, police station, court ... Ribz could never seem to break the cycle. It was as though every week he was getting nicked for something.

I can't count the number of times I went through it. I thought there was nothing I could do about it. I'm going away again. More time in jail.

It was generally the woman who was his foster carer who used to have to come to Brixton police station to deal with the formalities. It had been so long since he'd bothered to tell the police to contact his mother. He was glad that his mum wasn't there. In the early days she wouldn't turn up at all when he was nicked. And on the odd occasion that she did turn up, she used to arrive with 'fire in her eyes' and beat him in front of the police. He knew the whole situation with his mother was fucked up. That's why his exchanges with the police were much briefer.

'Where's your mum?'

'Don't know.'

'What's her address?'

'Don't know.'

'Where do you live?'

'Don't know.'

Birdie too had now got involved in the madness. He had learnt to drive and sometimes went with JaJa and Naja further afield to sell drugs and rob outside London. He was making loads of money. He met more and more criminals and drug pushers. But he never liked straying too far from home.

I always stuck close to home. Close to all these people like JaJa and Naj. There's history there. Like JaJa I know how he is. We may argue or whatever, but at the end of the day I know how he is, innit? I know his mum and that. I don't know them other guys' parents. That's how it is. I know Fat Si. I know all my people. That's why it's more like a family.

His views on prison hadn't changed. He never wanted to be put away, even when all the others were in and out of prison.

> *I see jail as a setback. As years out of my life. But because everyone was going to prison, it was a natural thing. I didn't think nufin' of it. It was what happened, weren't it.*

Then in 1999 things became difficult. There were disputes about money among some of his friends. There were always going to be conflicts. *People in Angell Town are, like, strong-minded. They're all wanting to get their views across*. Birdie wasn't argumentative. He shied away from conflict. He preferred to stay in the background. So when the arguments started he took a back seat. He spent more time with his girlfriend. She got pregnant and then had a miscarriage. It was a bad time. She became moody and depressed. He went through it all with her. He decided to retreat from the street and spend more time at home, away from Angell Town.

Chapter Twenty-four

Guns and Ammunition

I pleaded guilty to the firearm charge. I had it. A Smith and Wesson revolver. But as far as I was concerned I never shot no one.

Phat Si

The uniformed officials and plain-clothed CID who grabbed Fat Si when he stepped off the British Airways flight from Toronto pushed him into a prison van and drove him to Brixton police station. The charges were read to him. That's when he finally understood. He'd thought it might have somehow been forgotten. But it wasn't. It was about the guy who had been shot in the face outside the clubhouse in Angell Town.

The police said they had eight witnesses who said that Fat Si did it.

His head was in a whirl but he was pretty sure that he knew what had happened.

> *Someone has done something, I'm the easy target. I'm not*
> *living in the country. Normal thing to do. They are*
> *intimidated and blame it on me. Which they did.*

And he thought he knew who had grassed him up: an older guy
who he had looked up to. An older guy he was on the road with
had snaked on Fat Si to save his own arse.

> *I thought before, I want to be like this guy, but he was a pussy.*
> *Now he was showing himself to be even more of a pussy. That's*
> *when I decided, you know what, fuck everyone that's older than*
> *me, I wasn't going to follow the older boys no more.*

It was serious. Eight people had come forward to say that they
had seen Fat Si shoot the victim in the face. Many others had
made statements saying that he had a firearm.

> *From the day that the incident happened there were people*
> *saying that I did have a firearm. And I did have one. I'd just*
> *got it. I just had it. Someone gave it to me. I needed it to sell*
> *drugs. Not everyone had guns at that time. But I did. And*
> *my fellow gang banger had one too.*

Fat Si admitted that he shot the gun, a Smith and Wesson
revolver. But he never admitted that they were his bullets that
had hit the guy. But it was obvious what the police were thinking. The shooting had happened a few days before he left for
Canada. The police put two and two together. Fat Si had shot
the man, left the country and gone into hiding.

* * *

Inch was prowling around his cell in Brixton prison one day when, out of the blue, they brought in Fat Si. Inch hadn't seen him since the Angell Town shooting a couple of years back. He thought he was still living in Canada. His first thought was that Fat Si looked drawn out and stressed. Fat Si's first words to Inch showed just how anxious he was.

'Fucking hell, Inch, man. They're after me.'

Inch tried to reassure him but what could he say? He was there the day of the shooting. It was a pretty hectic day and things had got out of control. But he was convinced that it wasn't Fat Si who had put the bullet into the guy's face.

In November 1999, Fat Si was put on trial at the Old Bailey. Every morning he was taken from Brixton in a prison van, through the huge metal gates at the side of the Old Bailey to appear in a wood-panelled courtroom.

The prosecution presented its case. Several witnesses came forward to confirm they had seen Fat Si with a revolver. Eight people said they had seen him fire at Elijah Morrisson, the teenage victim. One of the rounds had ripped through the victim's face and lodged in his skull. The prosecution barrister explained that the bullet had missed the teenager's brain by an inch and that he was lucky to be alive. Surgeons had decided to leave the bullet where it was lodged.

But the statements were conflicting. Someone said that he had fired a total of twelve rounds. The firearm was never recovered. Fat Si knew that the witness statements didn't add up.

The police have not put me on no ID parade. They have recovered no shells from the scene. These people say that I let off twelve rounds. Everybody with common sense knows that a revolver does not have twelve rounds. Everyone with common sense knows that a revolver looks nothing like an automatic pistol. So people told lies.

Fat Si pleaded guilty to the firearm charge but not guilty to attempted murder. Now he needed support for his case.

Inch got the letter telling him that he had to appear in court one morning. He was making up his prison bed. He thought the prison officers were winding him up because he had gym that morning and they knew how much he hated missing it.

'No way am I going to go all the way there just to spend the whole day in court.'

'You've got to. You've got no choice.'

He sat for ages handcuffed in a witness cell waiting to be brought out. When he finally walked out into the courtroom he looked up and saw several people he knew in the public gallery. There was Fat Chris's brother. There was Gerry. There was Fat Si opposite him in the defendant's box. Inch sat down in the oak-panelled witness box. There was a hush in the courtroom. One of the court ushers hissed at him.

'Stand up.'

Inch didn't realize the microphone was on.

'Stand up for what?'

Stifled laughter ran through the courtroom. The judge turned on him.

'Can you please stand up, sir!'

They swore him in, asked his name, whether he could confirm that the man in the defendant's box was Simon Maitland, and how well they knew each other.

While one of the lawyers was talking he reached over for a glass of water on the bench beside him. There was more laughter in the courtroom. He had just stolen the judge's glass of water.

Inch said that he had been there when the man was shot and that it wasn't Fat Si who had shot him. He told them everything he knew.

'He didn't shoot nobody.'

Fat Si in the defendant's box felt the atmosphere in the courtroom change.

They couldn't believe that this little small guy would come in a courtroom and was talking with such bravado and act like this and he could not be lying. He had to be telling the truth. And it was the truth. I didn't shoot no one. D'you see what I'm saying? It was a comic scene. A black man drinking from the judge's glass.

On Monday, 22 November 1999, Fat Si was brought up from a cell in the Old Bailey to hear his fate.

The jury didn't take long to decide. He was found not guilty of attempted murder. But they did find him guilty of randomly shooting a pistol into a crowd of gang rivals.

The judge spoke up as he sentenced him.

'The word has to go out in Brixton that where people use guns, if you are convicted, you must be locked up. Gun law cannot be allowed to rule the streets.'

Fat Si was 19. He got 15 months.

Nobody was ever convicted of shooting Elijah Morrisson.

Chapter Twenty-five

Rapping, Robbing and Shooting

With JaJa, Inch and a couple of other brudders, I've never had an incident where I've had an argument with them. We've never come to blows. All my life I've noticed that there's not a lot of people I'm like that with. I've come to blows, all the time. Bare blows. But never with these guys. I saw the love from them. I trust my brudders. That's the time really and truly when I took the PDC serious.

Phat Si

Fat Si was out early in 2000. He'd been in custody for so long in the run-up to the attempted murder trial that he only had to serve a few months before he was released. It had been over two years since he had last been in Angell Town. He'd got out in the days following the clubhouse shooting and had never been back.

His first thought was the estate was much smaller than when he'd left. Pym House had been knocked down; Errol, Ribz's brother was no longer around; Inch's mum had moved out. *It's not the same. The estate has shrunk.*

Luckily JaJa was still there.

One day, not long after he'd been let out, Fat Si ran round to JaJa's flat in Marston House. He burst through the door and into JaJa's bedroom to surprise him. JaJa was lying there on his bed naked, fooling around with some girl. The poor guy jumped up and covered himself with a sheet, thinking he was about to be busted by the police for having dope on him. Fat Si noticed that there were pieces of paper by the bed. They had scribbles on them. Verses, rap verses.

'What ya doin' that for?'

'I'm writing stuff for the PDC.'

Fat Si looked blank.

'The Peel Dem Crew.'

Fat Si had heard about the Peel Dem Crew but he didn't really know what it was. He'd been in Toronto and in prison for so long that he felt as though he was out of the loop. He was intrigued, but he preferred to keep his distance. He didn't think he could rap.

On the sly side of things I always wanted to rap, but I didn't want to be a guinea pig in the rapping world.

He preferred to be 'on the kerb', doing his stuff, selling his drugs. He would let the others stick to the music and the rapping. He was happier on the road. That's how Fat Si first met Bloods.

* * *

Bloods was holed up in a safe house in Brixton. JaJa had found it for him and given him the keys. Bloods was lying low for a while. He was on the run. He'd been nicked by the police a few weeks earlier for attempted robbery but had got bail. He'd been nicked along with Solomon Martin, whose street name was Blacker. Blacker though had tried to escape from the court room itself. *If only he hadn't tried to escape he would have got bail too.*

Fat Si and JaJa used to leave food and money for Bloods on their way to the gym. That way he wouldn't have to spend too much time in the open. Those were bad times for Bloods but he kept himself going by writing more lyrics for his raps. The bars described his life and his world. He wrote bars about his dad who he didn't get on with. He called it 'Blood, Sweat and Tears'. He wrote lyrics about Quinney and JaJa and a girl called Zoe who always seemed to be there for him even when things weren't going well.

Fat Si was impressed. Even someone like Fat Si who struggled with the music could see that Bloods was talented. Bloods could write the words and rap them. He had an amazing memory which meant that the words would just stick in his head. Fat Si was glad that he had left the rapping to the experts.

But what most impressed Fat Si was the PDC. JaJa and the others kept him safe and sane and gave him money when he needed it. He realized that, even though he had always been in gangs, he now had something approaching a family.

* * *

The tranquillity didn't last long. Fat Si borrowed a postman's uniform off one of the 'cats'. At first he just wanted to show off. It was a laugh, walking around like a postman. He was always planning to give it back. But somehow he never did. Instead he decided to keep it and use it. He rented a car with a fellow gang-banger and drove to Essex. He had a plan. They found a Thomas Cook travel agent and parked the car round the corner. Fat Si undressed in the car and put on the postman's uniform.

He banged on the door of the bureau de change and one of the clerks, thinking he was dropping off some post, buzzed him in. Fat Si barged in and yelled at everyone.

'Get down, move to the back of the room.'

He ushered them all together, collected all their mobile phones and forced them to open the safe. He was hyped up and yelling at them. He knew how terrifying he must have looked to them – a big black guy yelling and threatening them. As the staff cowered on the floor he raided the safe and stuffed its contents in a bag. He came out of there with £40,000 in cash and another £20,000 in travellers' cheques.

He and his fellow gang-banger were high on adrenaline. They headed back to Angell Town feeling triumphant and rich.

But on the motorway they heard the whoop, whoop of a police siren. They pulled over. They had nowhere to run to. It was the Flying Squad. They had come after them. They searched the car and found everything: the money, the travellers' cheques and the postman's uniform.

He'd only been out of prison for a few months. Now Fat Si got sentenced again, this time for four years. The round of prisons began. First Feltham, then Wandsworth, his first experience of an adult prison, then Downview, Highpoint, Elmley, Swaleside, Stamford Hill …

A few weeks after that Bloods got re-nicked. He couldn't cope with being stuck in the safe house and had gone out hustling and robbing. That's when one of his co-ds, his co-defendants, had done a deal with the police. He'd snitched on him. Bloods was given two years. He wouldn't come out again until 2001.

Chapter Twenty-six

The PDC Come Together

It's not like going up to see someone and saying, 'Do you want drugs?' You have to hang around in the cold, and have a supply of drugs on a regular basis. It's not just buying it down the road. You have to find a regular supplier. It's cold, raining and you don't want to do it. It's so cold that you can't move. But you have to. Otherwise you are not going to have the money. Your girlfriend gets stressed out because you are on the road. They don't see what's going on in your mind. Drug dealing, it's not what it's made out to be. You wait for a whole day and you might only get two people.

JaJa

The first six months of 2001 were traumatic for Angell Town, and for the whole of the London Borough of Lambeth. Crime figures soared. In fact they were soaring through the United Kingdom. In 2001 there were a reported 22,300 gun crime offences in England and Wales, the highest figure on record. Police forces in Greater Manchester, Avon and Somerset and

Merseyside reported dramatic increases. In London, handgun offences tripled. And the London Borough of Lambeth was at the heart of the violence. In the first sixty days of the year, there were 1,200 muggings recorded in Lambeth, far higher than in any other London borough. The police had tried to stop the muggings by launching Operation Tippett. The plan was to put the Angell Town estate under overt surveillance to snare the muggers. But there were protests. Many in the local community rebelled against the plan and said it would provoke rioting. The police pulled the project. And the muggings continued. In May, an 86-year-old woman was mugged as she crossed Angell Town to return to her small flat on the estate. She died a few weeks after the attack. It was front-page news all over south London.

Outsiders had always avoided coming into Angell Town, preferring to walk right round the estate rather than cut through the middle of it. And in spite of the money pouring into the redevelopment of Angell Town the estate was as notorious as ever. JaJa's mum, Sharon Kerr, didn't only blame the gangs and the muggers.

It was the police who would also bring the war into Angell Town. It was the easiest way to get away from the police in Brixton. Drive into Angell Town. And the police would follow in their cars and on motorbikes. It was like America, like a war zone.

One day in July, the war came to her front door. A local man, a father of four, was shot dead by police marksmen outside her flat in Marston House. The man was brandishing a cigarette lighter shaped like a pistol. The policemen said they feared for their lives. Two of the bullets hit him in the back, the other two in the side. The policemen were never charged. The cycle of violence continued.

JaJa knew he was part of that cycle. Most of the money he got from drug selling came from 'dirty' money. *It's so dirty, it's filthy.* He knew that many of the muggings on the estate were carried out by crackheads looking to pay for their fix. JaJa knew that some of the crackheads even killed just to get their hands on money. *That money is evil. They get it from the worst places. Drugs are evil.* He knew all this, yet it didn't stop him from keeping up the drug-pushing operation from the stairwell and balcony of Marston House.

JaJa's drug-selling routine continued throughout 2001. He and others in the PDC would spend days 'on the block', in rain or shine, pushing out the drugs. He realized that it was exactly as it had been years ago when he was growing up. He remembered as a little boy leaning out of his kitchen window to listen to the 28s and the Yardie men hanging outside Marston House discussing their criminality. He remembered their conversations about drugs and 'tiefing' and realized that he was doing exactly as they did.

The drugs were harder, more potent, but otherwise it was the same system at work.

The PDC gang members would do shifts so they had the place covered most of the time. Sometimes there were only two of them standing around in the cold waiting for the 'cats' to arrive. Other times there were nine or ten of them on the first-floor landing. It was like running a business. Not only did he have to make sure he knew which suppliers would give him a reliable and regular supply, he also had to make sure the competition stayed out of the way.

That involved the English black boys from the PDC robbing from the Yardie Jamaicans to keep them away. The Yardies would hit back. The PDC would threaten them if they got too close. It was a continuous cycle of shootings and stabbings.

Sometimes the punters just wouldn't show. Sometimes he'd wait the whole day and make hardly any money. Sometimes it was so cold that you couldn't move. Sometimes it was boring. It was the only way that JaJa felt that he could make money. He didn't want to be a plumber or a carpenter or a bus conductor or work in McDonald's. He wanted to do what he'd always seen men do around him. He wanted to thieve and push drugs. And yet he couldn't really talk about it. It was not the right sort of thing to talk about. He was seeing a girl called Jemmy who lived on Brixton Hill but he felt there was too much going on in his head and that he couldn't really talk to her properly. He knew that his silence stressed her out too. And stressed-out girlfriends were just another headache.

One afternoon he got a call from Inch who was serving out his last year in prison. He was in a bad way. Inch had often called JaJa as he was being moved around from prison to prison. He hated being shunted around. The constant moving between cells and prisons just as you were getting comfortable and familiar with the place was the worst aspect of life inside. JaJa had tried to get Inch involved in rapping and had even written his first bar for him, but Inch found it hard. He was depressed. He was back in Portland and the racist abuse he was receiving from other prisoners was getting to him. He wanted to get out. He didn't know how much more he could take. He got JaJa on the phone and told him that he thought he was going mad, that life was too hectic and he was going crazy spending so much time in prison.

'Inch, man, those that do it young have more time to live life afterwards.'

JaJa's words eased him. *By serving my time now, I will have more to live for when I'm released.*

'When you get out, we'll sort it out. Don't worry, man.'

When Inch finally came out he had grown a beard. He was still short, but he was stockier and thicker set from the constant working out in the prison gym. As soon as they were together, JaJa told him of his plans to do something with his life.

JaJa's enthusiasm for life had always impressed Inch. He was always coming up with a new idea, a new way of making money. JaJa told him that he wanted the music to come off, but first he needed more money. There was not enough business in Angell Town. He needed to expand his patch. *If we branch out, we can make more money and then get the music business going.*

One day that summer, Inch and JaJa drove to Margate. JaJa had drugs with him. It was the first stage in opening up a new market on the south coast, a way of expanding business. But straight-away it went wrong. The police were waiting for JaJa as soon as he set up shop. JaJa suspected that someone had tipped the police off. Before the police could grab him, he hid the drugs.

They were taken to a police station. The police searched his car. They searched his bags. They searched him. They told him to strip and asked him to squat. One of the officers saw that he had a plastic bag dangling from his arsehole but still JaJa refused to hand it over. There was a scuffle that turned into a fight.

'If you don't give it to us, we're going to call a doctor who will pull it out.'

That made JaJa change his mind. He didn't want some doctor forcing his arse cheeks open.

'Here you are. Take it.'

JaJa was put on bail while the police investigated the contents of the package.

Birdie was still chilling but his money situation was messed up.

'Why's you don't get a job?'

After his girlfriend's miscarriage she was pregnant again and was on his case.

'I'm about to have a baby. You need to support us.'

The pressure stressed Birdie out but he got a job for six months at the Royal Mail.

The money was no good so he went out on the road again.

This time he got into cars. He learned from friends how to get rid of stolen vehicles. It worked well and he started making money again until one of his associates gave him a car that he said was clean. It was a nice car with a brand new satellite navigation system. Birdie knew the guy was lying and that the car was probably 'hot' but he presumed that his friend had covered his tracks and that Birdie would be able to drive it and not get nicked. He called up Inch and asked him if he wanted to go for a ride. Then they got chatting to some girls who were going to a rave. Birdie and Inch offered them a lift. It was an address on the Old Kent Road. They tapped the postcode into the on-board SatNav system and set off.

After a few minutes Birdie noticed that there was a cop car following them. He didn't think anything of it at first. So he switched lanes and went through an amber light. But still the cop car followed them. Suddenly, just as they were outside the girls' club, the cop car burst through a red light and cut them off.

'Stay where you are.'

They got out a torch and shone the light into Inch's and Birdie's eyes.

'This car is stolen.'

The girls in the back seat were pissed off. They were dressed up and looking forward to a party but they too were taken to the police station.

Birdie was charged with TDA – taking and driving away a stolen car. The charge didn't stick. The times that the police said he had stolen the car matched times when he had proof that he was on an education course. He was still given community service and a year's probation. Yet again he'd avoided prison.

Summer ended. The days got shorter. The nights got colder. It was the beginning of winter when Fat Si finally got out of prison. Even though it was cold, Fat Si turned up in Angell Town dressed in a 'wife beater' vest, showing off his muscled arms and broad chest. He was now 21 and felt strong and strangely primed for action.

I was a man now and in control and everything. This is when the gun thing is coming and it's gone mad now, innit, and I've jumped back into this ting on a hype now, I've come back to

Angell Town and I've jumped out of the car like an animal and I talk like a wild man. And everyone was greedy now, it was a nice environment and I loved it.

It was the first time in years that all the PDC had been out of prison at the same time. Everyone was there: JaJa, Inch, Naja, Sykes, Ribz, Biker, Birdie. The whole gang was back together. Rival gangs had moved on. It was the PDC who were well and truly in control of Angell Town. They were all bigger and stronger and older. Fat Si could no longer be called 'Fat'. He changed his street name to something he thought was more appropriate to his physique and his state of mind. Fat Si became Phat Si. It was slang from America meaning cool and fabulous. With his new name he was exhilarated by the prospect of the money they could make through criminality. *We are going to fuck up the roadside.*

Phat Si had spent most of his adult life in prison. Now he was out and free.

It lasted seven weeks.

Chapter Twenty-seven

The Raid on the Block

That was a serious, proper event. The police jumped out and
they were organized and we were organized. The police are
the biggest gang. They were a gang, we were a gang. It was
them against us, gang against gang. Marston House. That
changed everything.

JaJa

Birdie wasn't on the Marston House walkway that day in
December 2002 when the police raided it and caught Ribz,
Phat Si, Naja, Sykes and Skippy. He had been there earlier to hang
around with the others but by 3 p.m., when the raid happened, he
was out and about in another part of the estate. He'd heard Sean
Paul's 'Gimme the Light' through the open windows, he'd heard
the shouting and yelling, he'd heard the police sirens. But by the
time he got back to Marston House late in the afternoon his fellow
PDC members had all been taken away.

It wasn't as though he was surprised. There had been warn-
ings. One night he had even heard the police making a noise in

one of the flats that they'd taken over for surveillance. They'd even spoken to each other about the possibility of the police raiding Marston House. But while some of the PDC ignored the warning signs, Birdie made sure he trod carefully. He shied away from spending too much time around the block.

A flight to New York might have been what saved him. He'd booked to go and visit family there and as the date of the flight approached he made sure he stayed out of trouble. And that meant not hanging around the block too much.

Later that day, when the excitement was over and when the police had disappeared, he went up to the block and found out if anyone knew what had happened. He felt paranoid: he knew there was a risk that the police might come for him because he had been hanging around with the others over the past few weeks. The word on the street was that the police were after some people who had got away. People like Inch. But Birdie's name was never mentioned. He tried to chill and waited to hear if the police were after him.

Standing outside 124 Marston House once the noise and drama had died down, JaJa's mum, Sharon Kerr, began to burn with anger. From what she knew it was the first time that Naja had got involved so heavily in criminality. She blamed Elijah. She realized that she always blamed Elijah. Naja had got eleven O levels and was quieter and more sensible than Elijah. But Naja always looked up to his older brother and followed him. Elijah was his own man and could look after himself. But she wasn't so sure about Naja. That's why she watched Naja like a hawk.

She had always been firm with JaJa about the consequences of Naja following in JaJa's footsteps.

'If anything happens to him you are fucked, mate.'

She was also cross with herself. She had known the raid would happen. She always used to try and think ahead of the boys and warn them. That was the point of all those hours standing at the kitchen window looking at the comings and goings on the estate. She'd noticed things weren't right before the raid, a van that shouldn't be parked there, the twitch of curtains in the block opposite. She'd told JaJa and his friends a couple of days before the raid.

'Someone is watching you. Something's not right. Be careful.'

None of them listened to her. Now both her sons were in Brixton police station and she felt the familiar pattern of a long, drawn-out period of waiting descend upon her yet again. Days waiting in prison, weeks waiting for a court date, then maybe months visiting them in prison. She had been through it over and over again with JaJa and now it was starting again with Naja. She was upset. She always said it to herself but once again she repeated the same mantra.

'This is the last time. It's not going to happen again.'

The reaction on the estate was mixed. Some were glad that the PDC had been rounded up and taken away. Others who had lived on the estate all their lives and who had watched them grow up felt sorry for them. They still looked on them as a bunch of young kids.

The news of what happened on the estate reached Pod, one of the old guard from the 28s. He had moved out of Angell Town to live in Croydon where he was following in his father's footsteps and was training to be a pastor. He had moved on in his life. He was no longer part of the gang of 28s who used to educate the younger kids in the best ways to rob and sell drugs. In fact for the past couple of years, along with his father, he had tried to help JaJa and the others stay away from crime, but he knew there were limits to what he and his father could do. His father had told him how he had seen Phat Si the evening of the raid and had tried to persuade him to stay away from the commotion. But Phat Si hadn't listened.

> *My father always knew they were naughty. But he couldn't convert them. He realized he had no power to change their lives. But he understood their struggle. And they respected him as the local pastor. They often helped carry his shopping. And they would never do anything bad in his presence.*

While Pod couldn't condone the criminal life that JaJa, Phat Si and the others in the PDC had chosen, he also knew just how random the police actions could be. His own flat in Pym House had been raided by police four or five times. Once during a raid his father had flipped and angrily confronted the police. He asked them whether they really expected to find drugs or stolen goods in the house of a preacher. The police never really apologized but they did have an answer.

'We can't trust no one. Not even a vicar.'

In all their searches there, though, they never found anything.

In June 2003, JaJa was taken to the Inner London court for sentencing. He was up for two drugs charges – the Marston House case and the drugs bust in Margate. The results had come back positive from the drugs that he'd tried to stuff up his arse. His solicitor asked for the cases to be put into one and the judge at the Inner London court agreed.

JaJa pleaded guilty. What else could he do? They had him bang to rights. He'd been remanded in custody for six months, travelling back and forth between Margate, Canterbury Crown Court and the Inner London court, moving from prison to prison. He thought, during the endless hours of waiting, about pleading not guilty but the evidence against him was pretty strong.

> *If I pleaded not guilty and was found guilty I was looking*
> *at six or seven years. If I pleaded guilty I'm going to get five.*
> *I thought, man, I'm going to have to plead guilty and get*
> *the lowest I can.*

He sat in the downstairs holding area of the court with Sykes, waiting for sentencing. They were both nervous, discussing how much time they would get. JaJa was pessimistic. He had two cases pending and couldn't see any room for leniency. *I'm going to get five years.*

Sykes went up the stairs to the courtroom first. When he came down, there was a big smile on his face.

'I got twenty-two months.'

'What, is that it? You're lucky, man.'

'I'm going to be out next year.'

JaJa was called next. He went up the stairs to the courtroom. He felt like a condemned man. His stomach fluttered. *Oh no. I'm not looking forward to this.*

'Are you Elijah Kerr?'

The judge looked at him over his glasses.

'Yes'

'You've been arrested on several occasions. You are a repeat offender. You do not seem to be learning.'

JaJa feared the worst. He tried to defend himself. He told the judge that he was smoking crack and that he had to take drugs because life was so stressful. He had to sell drugs to support his habit. JaJa knew he was lying. He didn't have a drug habit but he didn't want to get five years. He made a big story out of it.

The judge began again, looking at JaJa's mother who was sitting in the courtroom with one of his sisters.

'Your family is here and they are trying to support you, so I am going to take what you have said into consideration.'

The judge sentenced JaJa to twenty-two months for the Marston House bust and eighteen months for the Margate bust. It gave him a total of three years, nine months.

Wow. I'll be out in fifteen months.

JaJa was pleased. He'd served some of it already. *Fifteen months. That's not so bad.*

For JaJa's mum the worst moment was when she had to sit there in court and watch a big screen with video footage of her two sons selling drugs. The same policemen who had repeatedly raided her house were giving evidence against them.

We sat there as mothers trying to defend our kids and the judge with his glasses on looking up at the screen and then looking at me and I'm like … ahhh.

She wondered where it had gone wrong. She didn't understand why her kids had chosen the ghetto way. She'd tried to protect them from it. She knew that her kids had seen her struggle, just like she had seen her parents struggle and suffer. It was a struggle that passed from generation to generation: a struggle to pay the bills, earn money, pay the rent. Now, she felt that JaJa was rebelling against it. Perhaps he wanted things differently. He rebelled because he didn't want to live the life she had led. And his way of rebelling was to get easy money.

No matter what I said or did, the more I gave Elijah the more he wanted. So it didn't matter what I did.

As she sat in court she went through their lives, thinking back on how she'd treated them. She'd always done her best to keep them clean and well fed. Even when she was holding down two jobs she'd always left her kids notes telling them what to do and how to look after each other. They always had an emergency contact number where they could call her at work. Even when she was working in the hospital or in an office they could still get hold of her. She thought back to the days when one of her colleagues, either Yasmin or David, would shout out to her.

'Sharon. It's one of your daughters on the phone.'

It was always said with a sigh.

Her daughter would be on the line.

'Mum. Naja's got the remote and won't give it to me.'

After Chantelle, Naja would call.

'Mum, Chantelle won't stop making a noise.'

Finally JaJa would call.

'Mum, Chantelle and Naja are messing the house up.'

Even though it was frowned upon to receive calls from home she still made sure that her kids could get hold of her. Every time she had to go off to solve a family problem she used to get funny looks. She didn't think that it helped that everyone knew she was a black single mum with four kids. She believed that some of her colleagues looked down on her.

But quite often the phone calls were of a more urgent matter. 'Mum. Someone's got shot outside our door.'

Then she would have to get permission from her boss to leave work and get back to Angell Town and try and get into her flat through the police lines and ambulances.

She was lucky that, once she had explained what sort of life she led, most of her bosses were pretty understanding. She'd had her first kid at 15, brought up four kids alone and lived on a rough estate with crack addicts and gunmen. That's why her bosses went easy with her and tried to help her out when they could.

When mobiles phones arrived it was a relief. She would put her phone on silent and sneak off into a corner when any of her kids phoned with a new complaint.

'Chantelle, just wait till I get home.'

She thought back to all she had done for them, the efforts she had made to be a good mum. Yet still JaJa ended up in trouble with the police.

In better moments, when Sharon had time and space to analyse these things, she didn't think that JaJa or his friends in the PDC were bad kids. She couldn't see them as violent criminals who would stop at nothing to get a new pair of trainers. She just saw them as a bunch of kids who were fighting racism, discrimination, alienation.

She believed that the education system had failed kids like her own. She'd never encouraged her kids to go to college or university. She didn't think they'd last five minutes. And she'd told them so.

'Don't go. It won't do you no good.'

She'd had the experience herself. She'd been to King's College in Waterloo and qualified as a psychiatric nurse. It was the murder of a good friend of hers, several years back, that persuaded her to get into the mental health profession.

It was 1994. Sharon had been working as a receptionist at Dolphin Square, near the Houses of Parliament. It was a place where MPs used to rent flats when they came to London from their constituencies. Her best friend there was a woman called Susan Shepherd. One day she got a terrifying phone call.

Susan had been murdered. By her boyfriend.

Sharon had heard all about him. His name was Michael Folkes. Susan used to pour her heart out to Sharon during their coffee breaks. He had moods and was unpredictable. Sharon never approved of the relationship.

But what she now discovered from the news bulletins was that Folkes had a history of mental illness.

He'd stabbed her seventy times and hit her over the head with a fire extinguisher.

The police later discovered bottles of prescription anti-depressant pills and tranquillizers lying unopened under his bed.

She wanted to know how the system had gone so wrong and so she decided to train as a care assistant at Guy's Hospital. Then, while she was at Guy's, she was offered the opportunity to train as a psychiatric nurse. She did placements at the Maudsley and Guy's and still managed to find time to go to the library during the day and do her mandatory hospital shifts in the evening. That was on top of running a home and looking after four raucous kids in Angell Town. At the age of 36, after three years of studying she qualified as a psychiatric nurse. But she'd been horrified by the uncompromising way in which she had been taught. She believed that the emphasis on classrooms and long lectures was blinkered. She found the teaching system too rigid. She believed it penalized single black women with kids like her. She'd found the whole experience difficult because it wasn't flexible enough to cater for individual circumstances.

It was one reason why she'd never pushed her kids into going into further education.

Chapter Twenty-eight

On the Run

*All I could think of was, where am I going next, where am I
sleeping tomorrow, how long can I stay in one person's house
before someone sees me? What if they don't like me? They
will snake on me.*

Inch

Inch was busy trying to stay out of sight after the Marston
House raid. While the others in the PDC were being moved
around from prison to prison and from court appearance to
court appearance, Inch was still on the run. He had only been
out of prison for a year and had no intention of going back. Two
months after the police raid he was still in hiding, staying with a
friend in Clapham.

He'd stayed away from Angell Town because he knew that
the local police would recognize him and nick him. Now he
knew he had to move again. He had to move to a different safe
house so that he didn't stay too long in one place. That's why
he decided to go to the shops to buy some credit for his mobile

phone so that he could let his friends and family know that he was on the move. But he was worried about being seen in the open.

His friend made him an offer.

'Don't worry. I'll drive you there. It'll be quicker.'

Inch agreed. *I'm driving. It's better than walking where anyone can see me. If I'm driving, I'm in a car and it will be safe.*

As they were driving through Clapham, Inch looked to the left and saw what he was sure were two 'feds' sitting in a car.

'You know what, you'd better find a road and drop me off.'

'Why, what's the matter?'

'I think there are undercover police officers back there and they've seen me.'

'Calm down, man, there are no feds.'

He looked back in the rear-view mirror and was sure that they were following him. Then another car drove towards them. He was sure they were checking him out. He was sure that the second car contained local undercover officers from Angell Town and that they'd recognized him.

'Listen, man, just drop me here and block the road so they can't chase me.'

The friend stopped the car but he didn't block the road. Inch got out and ran but he wasn't quick enough. Within seconds the police were on him.

'Get down. Down. Don't move.'

They shouted and yelled at him. Inch realized that they must have thought he had a gun on him. They held him in the car while they waited for the arrival of a local police officer who could confirm his identity.

Inch knew the officer. He was the only policeman who

regularly used to go into the estate and who'd known Inch since he was a little kid.

'Why didn't you warn me?'

The officer pointed out to him that he was a policeman and his job was to track down criminals.

Nevertheless, Inch felt a strange sense of betrayal.

They took him to Brixton police station. *Fuck this shit.* His heart sank when the judge sentenced him a few months later. He got three years.

When Birdie heard what had happened to Inch he made sure he bought a new car with tinted windows.

Chapter Twenty-nine

Life Inside

At the end of the day, I will go back to Angell Town and, without the excitement, it will be lonely. And if you're lonely in Angell Town, it's the worst.

JaJa

Inch was sent to Brixton prison. It was his first time in an adult prison. He felt tears come to his eyes. He'd just done a five-year stretch in various institutions and he'd been out on the road for hardly a year and now here he was back with another long stretch ahead of him. Unlike some of the others who seemed to accept their fate, the early days of prison always rocked Inch badly. For several days he was numb and scared, tears constantly forming in his eyes.

He was relieved when he found out that JaJa, Phat Si and Skippy were all in there with him. JaJa gave him some supplies, cornflakes, Frosties and stuff, and the others from the PDC made sure that he had everything he wanted.

We had some links in jail, obviously, innit? They see you are decent people and you get stuff. D'you get me? Other times you see people that got stuff that you need so you nick it.

It was the closest he had to a family in there. Nevertheless he became tearful again when he thought that the last time they had all seen each other was when they had all been free.

'It could have been worse. You might have got five years. You'll be OK.'

That's what JaJa said to him. There were four of them sitting in the cell in Brixton prison. It was 'association' time. It meant they had an hour's free time when the doors of a prison wing were open and they could walk into each other's cells, chat and catch up with each other. JaJa could see how stressed Inch was. Because Inch had been caught later than the others he had still not adapted to the rhythm of life inside. And seeing Inch stressed just made JaJa even more stressed.

JaJa could see the tears welling up in Inch's eyes. He hoped he wouldn't start blubbing in front of everyone. He feared it might set him off too. *Oh no. Please don't cry.*

For Inch, talking to JaJa and the others made it better. He could never let his friends down but he always felt that he had upset his parents. His dad didn't talk to him much and wouldn't come to visit. His mum came to visit because she lived so close to Brixton but as they sat opposite each other it was awkward.

She can't hide her disappointment in me.

Bloods soon joined them in prison. He'd got out in 2001, but a year later he was back in again. It was his friend who had persuaded him to rob the bar. The friend had gone into the bar with a gun and tried to open the safe while Bloods waited outside as the getaway driver. When the police came the friend snitched on him and he too was found guilty. He got five years for armed robbery.

During his first months in Brixton prison, JaJa was once again haunted by the thought that he was missing out on life on the outside.

> *I'm wasting my life. What am I doing here again? I was pissed off and I hated that time. The older you get the more you have to lose.*

When he came out he would be 24. He was getting older, he had no kids and he'd done nothing with his life.

He realized that he'd lost the chance to be with his girlfriend, to hang out with the people he loved. He might even lose his girl. It was a bad and stressful time. When the screws ordered him around he got really pissed off. It had been different when he was younger. He hadn't minded being pushed around so much, but now that he was older he wanted some respect.

'I'm a big guy now so you got to talk to me better.'

The prison officers just slammed the cell door in his face. JaJa took it personally. He spent most of his time being angry. The screws just laughed at him. The worst part was that they put him in cells with big, old men, rather than his young mates.

Once he was put in a cell with an old Portuguese guy, a crackhead who stunk so much because he didn't wash and who muttered and farted and acted crazy.

One night the old guy wouldn't stop shaking and itching and muttering.

'Shut up, you crackhead. Shut up or I'll batter you.'

The threats didn't stop the old man.

JaJa got so mad that he smacked the old guy round the face repeatedly until he shut up. He threw a blanket over the old man's face to cover up the blood and the bruising and went to sleep on the top bunk. When the cell door opened in the morning the old man scuttled out of there as quickly as possible. JaJa never saw him again. The prison officer looked at him with a strange sort of smile.

'You're bloody lucky that he didn't say it was you who did it.'

Each time he came back from a court appearance he was put in a new cell, sometimes by himself, sometimes with a rapist or a murderer. If the prison officer was a decent sort he would try and give JaJa the same cell he'd been in before. That was the worst part of it. The constant changing of cells and prisons. The constant long journeys in prison vans. The constant having to readjust to a new system and to new inmates who would stress him out in different ways. One of the worst was a guy who was about to be deported. He spent all his time in his cell crying and wailing to JaJa about how he was going to be taken away from his wife and his kids. It freaked JaJa out but made him even more aware of the importance of family and friends.

If only he could stay in Brixton. If only he could stay close to where the PDC was well known and respected. Instead, he was sent all over the United Kingdom. From Canterbury in Kent, to the far corner of Wales. Fortunately, at each jail there was always someone he knew from back home in Angell Town.

The first few months in prison for Phat Si were hellish. He felt himself going crazy. He got into fights until they put him in basic. It meant he was by himself, in segregation, with no television at all, 24/7. He had a job at the servery but in the evening he would end up in his cell, lying on his bed by himself, smoking weed and thinking too much. Over-thinking.

I would sit in my cell and things would go around my head. I was thinking, why am I here? Why am I in jail? Why has God done this to me again? I started thinking that there was a higher power that was watching me and locking me up and that. I wonder if I will ever get out. I was just getting paranoid and that. I thought the screws were listening into my conversations. I thought people were listening to me. I was over-paranoid.

He felt that his family was falling apart. He felt that he was falling apart. Phat Si began to hear voices pursuing him at night when he was alone in his cell. He began to think that people were talking about him. He didn't know it at the time but he seemed to be teetering on the edge of a schizophrenic breakdown.

Inch and JaJa saw it happening.

JaJa first noticed it when he used to come past Phat Si's cell during association time. Because Phat Si was not allowed out, it was the only time he could talk to him. Through the small hole in the prison door he could see tears forming in the corner of Phat Si's eyes and hear the tremble in his voice. He talked to Phat Si constantly about the posse, about the future, to keep him from going under.

'Stay focused. There are bigger things we can do with the PDC when we get out of here. You're not going to stay here forever. PDC. There are bigger things waiting for us.'

But each time he heard Phat Si's voice break, it stressed out JaJa even more. *Why is everyone crying? Please don't cry. Please don't cry, brother.*

It was JaJa's support that kept Phat Si sane.

It's like he opened his arms and brought me into the family.
If it wasn't for JaJa I think I would have gone off my rocker.

It took three months but gradually he began to understand that you can never find right answers. *No one finds those answers. That's how life is. That's the way it is.*

Then one day, his mum came to visit him in prison. She'd flown in from Canada. He didn't know that he was going to get some answers to the one question that had haunted him his whole life. *Why did you leave me behind when you went to Canada?*

She sat down opposite him in the visitor's room and began to talk.

It was the same story that he'd always heard in his community.

You got a young, attractive strong black man with a family
and there are a lot of women out there. There is a lot of
temptation, innit? My dad was fucking all over the place
and she couldn't stand it. He was fucking about. He was the
man of the moment. She's not stupid. She's not ugly. My

*mum was a beautiful woman and couldn't take it. She
could still do better than that so that's what she done.*

She told him about the day when he was eight years old and he
had come back to find the family home in Stockwell empty. She
told him that she had wanted to take him with her, but his father
had begged her to leave him behind.

'Don't take my only son. Leave him here with me.'

That's why she had flown to Canada with his sisters but had
left him behind. She wanted to take him. Honest she did.

For Phat Si, hearing the story for the first time was the first
time he'd had facts.

*She opened the book and told me everything. It doesn't
matter if it was nice or not. It was an eye-opener. It was
reality. It was facts.*

If there was resentment, he'd buried it. He'd been independent
for so long. It had become part of his life. He'd grown up not
having anybody looking after him, not having anybody
around. For him, it was normal that nobody knew where he
was. He was always on the streets. Even from as young an age
as eight.

Things got better after that. He felt as though he was regaining
some sanity. JaJa was around; he knew how long he was going to
be in prison and the PDC encouraged him to start rapping. *I'm
shit, but I'm going to get there. Anyone can do what they want in life.
I'll get there. I'll make it.*

He wrote PDC graffiti on the prison walls and felt like he
was part of a brotherhood. Soon he was ducking and diving in

prison like before. He managed to get hold of mobile phones and would send photos of his dick to his girlfriends. They in turn would send him pictures of their breasts or the vibrators called 'rampant rabbits' up their pussies.

I was walking round the exercise yard with a mobile phone to my ear going, 'What's up, man?' or 'What's up, darlin'?' I had girls everywhere, man.

He was caught with illegal mobile phones and sent to solitary. But that didn't stop him getting hold of more mobile phones.

JaJa was moved to Canterbury prison in Kent. He'd heard rumours that the prison was racist. Now he experienced it at first hand. There, the inmates played a racist game of pool. The idea was to try and get the black ball in the pocket. Every time the black ball fell in the pocket the white inmates would cheer and shout.

'The black ball goes.'

JaJa knew it was a way of intimidating him, but another black guy from Brixton and a white guy from Essex, who JaJa got on well with, told him not to worry.

'They're racist and they'll talk but they won't touch you.'

And no one did.

He began to think about his dad for the first time in years.

I started wishing my dad had been there with me. I started asking myself questions. Where was he all those times when he should have been looking after and protecting me?

He began to realize what a struggle it must have been for his mum, bringing up four kids by herself. There was never enough money, no food in the cupboard, no money to pay the phone bills.

He thought about his life and the choices he had made.

At school they'd told him he could be a fireman, a policeman, a nurse. *That was about it. That's about all the opportunities you are given.* But he didn't have a fireman, policeman or doctor living next door. He had robbers and muggers and drug dealers and drugs always won out. The excitement, the girls, the money involved with drug dealing were just too powerful.

But now, without all that, he felt different. He felt bored.

That's when you realize you have no one but yourself. I am by myself in this world, even though I've got a family that I love and that love me. End of story. All I have is myself. If you know that, you can be a better person. You don't need to rely on people.

He had time to think and he had time to blame someone. And he began to blame 'the system'. He couldn't quite formulate the argument but he reckoned there was something in the way his world worked, something to do with parents, police, teachers, social workers, local and national governments, something in 'the system' that was meant to trap young men like him. He believed that people like him and Phat Si and Ribz and Inch couldn't get out of places like Angell Town. *The door out of the 'hood is never open to people like me.* The 'system', he believed, with the police as its shock troops, victimized him. He thought back to the rich white men he used to buy drugs off and wondered why they never seemed to be the ones put on trial. And his resentment against 'the system' grew.

The police are just a big gang. That's why I don't have nothing to do with them. They cover it up by following petty people that are down on the bottom of the ladder. We go to jail and do big sentences when the guys that are doing the crimes are the powerful people.

That's when a new interest began. He'd heard about it on the streets on the outside but had taken no interest. Now, in all the prisons he'd been sent to, particularly in Brixton, people were talking about it and getting into it. The speeches were powerful; the books had meaning for him. It became more and more a part of prison life. JaJa found inspiration there. Islam began to take hold of his life.

Chapter Thirty

Inch in Brixton

*In prison, nothing changes. You are left alone with your
thoughts. And that can be a good thing. But it can also be a
bad thing.*

Inch

I nch was too preoccupied to think of religion. He would think
about anniversaries: the dance they'd organized on a certain
day a year ago, the music event they'd been to, the takeaways
they'd had, the girls he'd been with. He badly missed all those
things he couldn't have.

He missed girls. He missed sex. He tried to be friendly with
the women staff because he knew that you could steal time in
prison to have sex with the English teacher, or the librarian, or
the dinner server. The women staff liked him. His girlfriends
wrote letters to him. One of them, Aleisha, came to visit. It was
possible 'to get busy' during visiting hours but not have full-on
sex. He fantasized about having sex without having the screws
rush you.

Sitting alone at night in his prison cell he began to re-evaluate his life. He remembered that the last time he'd been in prison he'd said that enough was enough.

I thought, I'm never coming here again, and I said it all the time, I remember thinking, 'I said this last time and here I am again,' and I'm back in fucking jail with people talking to you like you are a piece of shit. You think about everything you've just left on the road.

He thought about his upbringing. He was different from Phat Si or Ribz or even JaJa in that he had two stable parents. His dad and his mum had always been there for him if he really needed them. But even though he had a stable family with parents who had instilled some values in him, he still had his struggles. He wondered whether having a stable family life was overvalued. With two parents the hassle from them was just doubled up.

I used to get two sets of beatings. That was the only difference. Slap, slap. Tchh. Tchh. I used to get beatings the whole time. Proper beatings with belts and slaps. Beatings that go in time with the words.

Then on other days he would suddenly miss his mum and dad and his brothers and sisters. He missed normal life.

When you don't have it, you miss it.

He remembered how it had been the last time he'd been in prison. He'd spent so long living within the confines of an institution that expectations of what life would be like on the outside were exaggerated and unrealistic. He'd imagined that he would be able to come out and get things moving, have a big car, dream up a brilliant idea, make money, go straight and make things happen. It didn't work like that. In the end his brilliant plans for the future had crashed and burned and he'd ended up back in prison.

When you are in jail you only think about what you are going to do. You don't think about what is going to stop you doing it. You don't think about what everybody else is doing. When you're in jail you think, I'm locked up and I can't do this or can't do that so when I get outside I'm gonna appreciate it and I'm gonna do this and do that. You could wanna be straight but how do you get to actually do that? You don't know how hard it is to do that.

He thought about the two years he still had to serve. Once again he made up his mind, as he always did. He was going to be more realistic with his expectations. When he finally got out he wasn't going to get carried away.

This is the last time I'm in prison. Next time I'm out, I'll stay out.

Chapter Thirty-one

Islam

We are against the system and that's why everyone came to Islam. And what was happening in the prisons was happening on the streets.

JaJa

JaJa's move from Brixton to Canterbury had unsettled him. He plunged deeper into his thoughts. There were certain questions that JaJa wanted answers to and now he realized that neither Rastafarianism nor Christianity had ever really helped him. He knew he was a God-fearing person. He'd felt it since he was a young kid. He'd always known that there must be some powerful being that had thought of creating the amazing things of life: eyelashes to keep stuff out of your eyes, fingers to hold things with, a rounded foot so that you could walk properly. But nobody had ever managed to answer his questions to his satisfaction.

If weed grows on a grave in a churchyard, does that make it OK to smoke it?

He always asked questions like that and was always unhappy with the answers he was given.

When he was younger he went to church but never really got the vibe. He read the Bible loads of times but it never felt right. It never got into his head.

Everyone else is clapping and happy and I am the odd one out. I don't feel the same things. I don't feel no vibe. I don't wrong no one's beliefs but it didn't work for me.

He had the sense that adults deluded themselves, that they said and did certain things on a Sunday, then contradicted themselves the rest of the week, by drinking wine, or chasing women, or cussing their wives.

So when he was moved from Canterbury to Pentonville in north London and met a Muslim guy who told him about the Muslim way of life, he was ready to listen.

Ribz too had begun to think more deeply. He began to think about his life. He'd seen dealers and crackheads do terrible things to his mother and to his brothers. A year earlier he'd watched his oldest brother, Skippy, teeter on the edge of some terrible drug oblivion. Skippy was four years older and had always wandered further afield than Ribz. He'd watched Skippy get more and more hooked on crack to the point where he was living on the streets. People on the estate began to gossip about him being a junkie. That hurt Ribz. But it hurt him even more when he was wandering through the West End one day and came across his brother. His brother was dressed scruffily in a long, black Puffa jacket even though it was a baking hot summer's day. Ribz tried to avoid him. He was with some others and didn't want to be seen with him, but his brother came up to him and hugged him.

'How are you doin', bro?'

Ribz could hardly stand the smell. His brother stank. He hadn't washed for weeks. Ribz realized he was in a drugged-up stupor. He tried to shake him off and immediately felt bad that he was disrespecting his eldest brother. He felt tears come into his eyes. He was angry with his brother because his mind was too weak to get off the crack. There were some people who managed to smoke and maintain some standards but his brother no longer had any control over how he was living.

That crushed my heart, seeing my brother like that. I looked up to him and it made me mad seeing him. That's what he's become and the paparazzi and everyone was talking about it and when a person turns weak, people start exaggerating and people put you down differently. They can't put you down physically so they are going to break you down mentally.

The estate was rife with rumours about Skippy becoming a junkie. Ribz thought he heard people whispering behind his back. It was as though those who Ribz nicknamed 'the paparazzi' were spreading the news all over Angell Town that Ribz's brother was weak and feeble.

That was a turning point for Ribz. It made him stronger. He swore that he would never go down the route of hard drugs. The most he would ever do was sniff the air when someone nearby was smoking crack. Otherwise he stayed well clear.

Where will it end? That's the question Ribz asked about his brother, his mother, all his family members. It was the question he asked about himself.

He was still only 20 but he'd already been through a lifetime of trouble. He wanted to change a lot of things in his life. So when one of the inmates in Onley prison gave him some books and some tapes about Islam he was ready to read, listen and change.

Truth hurts, innit? What I mean by that is when I listen to it, it made me cry, innit? Something's hurting. That's when you know that you are blind to the truth, yeah?

In prison his Muslim brothers taught him that no one is perfect, that God likes people who sin and repent. That's why God made the world imperfect. That's why Ribz had done things wrong in his life. It made him feel better; the knowledge that he could still repent, that he still had time. He began to go to the prison mosque and gain knowledge by reading the Koran. *I'm beginning to understand things, to understand what my life is about, what I'm living for.*

He began to appreciate jail.

He felt as though he'd wasted a quarter of his life, but now he could make it better.

If I'd never went I wouldn't have seen the things I've known today. Jail is a place for you to understand yourself, to control myself. It's the only time you can sit down and know the mistakes you've made. D'you know what I'm saying? You can change those mistakes and make it right. Everything happens for a reason, innit?

He thought that if he hadn't been in prison he might be dead through all the crazy things he'd done. He might have killed someone. Someone might have shot him. Being inside slowed him down.

Some people on the outside don't understand. They live for money. Islam makes me understand that there is more to life than this.

He listened to more and more tapes that he got from some of the prison preachers. There was one particular tape that he played over and over. It spoke of how the Masons betrayed the Christians in order to rule the world. The tape explained that Muslims had a mission. They had to stop the growing Masonic influence. That influence even appeared in popular culture. Another preacher gave him a tape of a Madonna song. When he played the tune backwards he believed it showed that she was singing about devil worship. That made Ribz think how deep life and religion were and how, if misused, it could corrupt.

There is only one way really and that way is through Islam.

That's what made more sense to him than anything. That's what his Muslim brothers told him and that's what made him convert to Islam.

He became more and more convinced that British society was corrupt. When things finally went good for him he knew he needed to go abroad and live his life.

There is nothing for me here. Over here is just full of corrupt. Over here is poison.

In Pentonville, JaJa was also getting a vibe from a Muslim brother. He started reading Islamic texts off his own back. JaJa couldn't understand why they needed to pray five times a day but the guy had an answer for everything.

'God has given us so much. It is good to give him thanks.'

JaJa liked the idea of giving thanks. He liked the idea of being clean. Cleanliness is next to godliness. JaJa had always been a clean person. He liked things to be neat. He liked his body to be clean. He liked discipline and cleanliness. He hated dirt. It was something that struck him as being right.

'Ask for forgiveness. Ask for things to be provided for you. Prayer is personal. Just you and God.'

The more the guy talked, the more he felt drawn to Islam. He liked the idea of a personal relationship with God. *It keeps you focused within yourself.*

'At the end, it's not you and your family, or you and your crew, or you and the PDC. It will be just you and God.'

JaJa slowly felt his view of his world shifting.

It opened up my eyes to a lot of things. I saw the speed of life, the scattiness, the way we were living. I'm used to getting easy money. So, it's hard. There is temptation every day. You can't have this lifestyle without getting tempted.

The discussions in prison got political. There was talk of the terrorist plane attacks in America. There were some prison preachers who talked of the Taliban in Afghanistan and how their activities were affecting life in the West. They talked about Islam and how some kids were attracted to it for the wrong reasons. They were attracted by rebellion. But that too struck a chord with JaJa. Rebellion was attractive. He wanted to be part of a movement, to rebel against the system. The more he heard about the uncompromising culture of the Taliban the more he liked some of the ways they did things. He liked their hardness, their strong beliefs. He liked the way they stood up to the Western system and challenged it.

Rebellion is attractive. The Taliban and all that. The goodness of religion. This is what they feel they are about. We wanted to be part of a movement and a rebellion. You are hitting up the system. And lots of people don't like the system.

JaJa was hooked. Islam was his future. He prayed and read and went to lectures in prisons. Some of the lectures were given by radical preachers who were pretty hardcore. JaJa wasn't sure how to react to their exhortations.

'Kill the kaffirs. Jihad is the way.'

There were some in prison who wanted to go to Pakistan to learn how to make a bomb. There were others who spoke of bombing the London Underground.

But there were also opposing views. Many Muslims in prison rejected violence. They talked of peace and understanding.

'We have to live in peace with other religions. We don't have to cross each other's paths. We don't have to believe what they believe but we can leave each other alone.'

In Brixton and Pentonville the split views had caused some tension. There were some preachers in prison who were worried about the radical Islamists and took time to warn JaJa away from them.

'They will try and brainwash you. Stay away from that

brother. He will pollute your mind. It's best to go your own route. It's best to learn your own way.'

The problem was that he found it hard to go down his own route. He had never felt British. He just lived in England. He felt it was always a strange place and he wanted to get out as soon as possible. It pissed him off that he felt as though he had to live the way he did. He felt as if he'd had no choice. He'd only seen one road. He'd been involved with drug dealers and that's the road he'd taken.

He realized that in one sense he was lucky.

I could have talked to a crackhead first and become a crackhead. Or a rapist and now I'd be a rapist. Or a killer. That's what the streets are about. There was no one really for me to turn to. If I'd met like an internet wizard I would have been OK. But I didn't. I met a burglar.

It was hard to tell whether it was Islam or prison that began to turn things round for JaJa. He began to realize certain things about himself that he hadn't realized were there.

My comfort is bigger than everyone else's. Everyone else is trainers and cars and watches and they are all right. If they get it now they are fine. I'm not comfortable with that. I need more things. I want like bigger things, my ambitions are more bigger, more solid. I wanna aim big. That's why I'm attracted to a bigger level so we can make bigger money.

What kept him awake at night was the thought that, in a few years' time, unless he sorted himself out, he might be back in prison again seeing the same faces he had known when he was in jail the first time.

> *I didn't wanna go back to prison. I didn't wanna get back in that cycle of keep coming back in. When I was in there I saw the same people that I was in jail with the first time, the whole same people, we were like, 'Remember when I see you when you were 16'. I was thinking na, I don't want to be like this seeing you again when I'm thirty. 'Hello mate, how long are you doing now?' I said forget that. That's why I've got to do something else to make money. Something straight.*

That's when he knew that he had to start making some serious money through music and that if he wanted to think of the PDC on a business level he would have to start planning it straightaway.

When he was moved to Highpoint prison in Suffolk he calmed down and made himself more comfortable. It was an old RAF base and the regime there seemed to be less harsh. It was designed to help prisoners prepare for their release. JaJa took business classes from morning till night. He learnt accountancy and how to write a business plan. It was a five months course and he passed it easily. At night in his cell he started mixing street music and rap. That's when PDC Entertainments was born.

Chapter Thirty-two

Murder

I got friends in jails for shootings and murders. One of my friends is in jail for shooting someone in the head. It was over a petty argument. Sometimes there will be two crews and someone from that crew might rob someone from that crew, and someone from that crew might retaliate by shooting that person. That person might die, so the other crew might kill someone. There's a rivalry there, and over the years people get shot and die. You can't talk about these things coz there are still rivalries that go on till this day. That's basic street life stuff.

JaJa

The biggest event of Ribz's life happened a few weeks after he came out of prison. It was the end of November, 2003. He was back in Angell Town, trying to get his life together. He'd left Brixton and was driving through West Norwood with some of his PDC brothers talking about Islam and stuff. They had no idea they were being followed. They'd just turned a corner when several cop cars appeared out of nowhere and cut them off. Armed police jumped out and surrounded them.

'Get out the car. Get out the car.'

Ribz had no idea what was going on. He got out of the car and the screaming started again.

'Get on the floor. Get down.'

As they knelt on Ribz's back, they handcuffed him.

'We are arresting you for murder.'

They took him to the police station and interviewed him. Someone had been shot dead on Brixton Road and the police had a tip-off that it was Ribz who had done it.

When Ribz was put on an ID parade a girl picked Ribz out as the shooter.

This is a life sentence for me.

He went to court fearing the worst. But there was a miracle and he thanked Allah for it. After hearing the evidence the judge summoned the jury. He said that they would have to find Ribz 'not guilty' because the main witness, the girl, kept changing her story and wasn't making sense. She had said in her first statement that it wasn't Ribz who had pulled the trigger. Then she made another statement going back on the first statement saying that it was Ribz. She explained that she had kept quiet at first because she feared that Ribz would send people round to her mum's house to do her harm.

The change of story didn't go down well with the judge.

It was a massive relief, a weight off Ribz's shoulders. He wasn't set free, though. Ten rounds of ammunition had been found in the car he'd been travelling in and he was sent straight back to Belmarsh prison. This time, though, he didn't cry when he was locked up again. After all the years of being put away he'd become immune to it. This time he just went back to his cell, lay down and closed his eyes hoping that it would all end well.

For Ribz it did work out OK. Now that he had got off the murder charge the prison governor said that he'd only have to serve a few more weeks.

When you think to yourself you are never going to see the outside again that is a big thing. A major thing. It's the most serious thing you can ever go to jail for, innit? Murder and attempted murder. But by the grace of Allah …

Ribz went back to the trauma of life inside. Outside too, the trauma continued. Over the next few months, gun crime would haunt everyone associated with Angell Town and the PDC.

On 13 April 2004 there was a shooting outside the bagel shop on the Walworth Road just down the street from Angell Town. The victim was taken to hospital. He died there later that day. His name was Justyn Morgan, a kid that JaJa and the others had all grown up with and who hung around with the PDC crew. The news of the slaying reached JaJa in prison. He was shocked. He had no idea who would want to kill Justyn. And the police had no formal suspects. JaJa vowed to produce something positive out of the tragedy. What he didn't realize from his prison cell was that the streets of Angell Town weren't the same any more. Life outside was changing. Some of the younger PDC members were beginning to drift away from the PDC to form their own sub-group. The police and media gave the new group a nickname. The Muslim Boys. The word on the street was that their influence was growing. And most in the community thought that was a very bad thing.

Chapter Thirty-three

Tempman

*I loved those days. 'Tempman, Tempman'. I wanted to be
the biggest ever. I wanted to be the best that there was ever.
I wanted to be the baddest that there was ever.*

Tempman

Tempman was born Darren Samuels in 1987. The origins of
his street name were obscure. Even he didn't know quite
where they came from. It started as Temptation, Temperature,
then Temptastic. He was having fun with the word 'Temp'.
Finally he was play-fighting with a friend of his.

'Temp, man. Temp, man. Leave off.'

From then on it was Tempman. He was 14 years old.

He was born in Deerdale Road, Herne Hill, just up the road
from Angell Town. He didn't spend long there. His mum was
on crack so when Darren was three years old she put him and
his sister into a children's home.

When it was time for someone to foster him he had come
down with chickenpox. He scratched and scratched himself to

stop the itching. Nobody picked him. His sister found a place, but they didn't want to take a boy. In the end, a woman he called 'Aunt' Sissie in Croydon agreed to take him in.

It was a couple of years before his real aunt, his mother's sister, who lived in Brixton, agreed to look after both Darren and his sister. His aunt, though, laid down one condition. He had to take his schooling seriously. He was sent to Jessops primary school in Brixton. On his first day, his aunt gave him a warning.

'If you get expelled I'm not having you no more.'

That's when he met his dad. He was playing outside his auntie's house. His mum had come for a day visit. A big black man walked up and gave Darren £4. As the man walked away, Darren's mum turned to him.

'That's your dad.'

That was the first and last time Darren Samuels ever saw his father.

Darren lasted a couple of weeks at Jessops primary school. He was expelled almost immediately. He fought and caused trouble. His aunt wouldn't listen to any excuses. She'd told him what would happen if he got expelled. She kicked him out and he was sent to another foster home near Angell Town. He was miserable there. They used to dress him up in old cast-off clothes that were musty and didn't fit. He rebelled by punching the other kids in the home.

They wanted to turn him into a good Christian and he would spend hours in some Christian centre. The only thing he got out of it was a taste for dunking biscuits in his tea until there was more soggy biscuit than liquid in his cup.

When they couldn't cope with him he was sent to a school

for kids with behavioural difficulties. The Abeng Centre was opposite Brixton police station. It didn't change him. He caused havoc by fighting, spray painting, writing graffiti and stealing. So they sent him back into the children's home. That didn't work either. He was out of control, smashing things up, fighting staff and screaming and throwing stuff at them. Whenever he could he would dip into the petty-cash tin and make off with the money to buy food just to fill his hungry stomach. And he would stay out late. He just didn't want to go home.

Sometimes he stayed out all night long with his friend Marvin. 'Marvellous', Darren Samuels called him. Others called him 'Wild' Marvin. They used to 'roll' together, spending their time in the arcades in Brixton or stealing food from Woolworths or Safeway's. Darren was permanently hungry. The foster home gave him £5 a week but he would often spend all his money on the first day on sweets and other food. That's why he had to steal stuff the rest of the week. A whole gang of them would go into supermarkets and fill their pockets. There were so many of them that they never really got caught. He'd eat what he nicked but it didn't satisfy him. He was always hungry.

One night as he and 'Marvellous' roamed further down the Brixton Road, he came across a new estate. He was taken aback by the big buildings with yellow doors and long corridors that linked all the buildings on the estate together. It was kind of dark and forbidding. He didn't know it, but he was in Angell Town, right outside Marston House. Rather than go home he and 'Marvellous' got stoned. They spent that night in a 'dumpster', a rubbish skip, just round the back of Marston House. That's how much he didn't want to go back to the foster home.

Nobody could cope with him, so Darren was shipped out to Margate. Most of the kids in the new children's home were white and from a different background to him, but he managed to have some fun times there. It was mad. He rolled with the white kids, got plaits in his hair and got into Jungle music. He even started MC-ing at a few raves. His sister came to visit and he enjoyed showing her round. It reminded him that he had a family of sorts. He was there for two years.

Then he got moved again. This time to Catford in south-east London. He was pleased. He was getting closer to his family, such as it was.

At weekends he used to leave Catford and head for Brixton to meet up with his cousin and his friends. He knew a lot of them from his time at Jessops primary school before he had been expelled.

That's when he became Tempman. That's when he graduated to terrorizing people. There was something about his name and manner that intimidated people. Tempman and his mates would just go out into the streets of south London and nick mobile phones and handbags.

He now had his own 'bredren', friends who went by the street names of Turfer and Messy. They used to criss-cross London, obsessed with watching girls and robbing.

'Hey, there are bare girls over Croydon.'

It's what one of them would say. It meant that there would be a lot of girls to look at in Croydon.

They would get on the bus and hang out there, eyeing up the girls in their low-cut tops. They went to the bus station, a favourite hang-out place where all the local school kids seemed to meet. That's when they would run riot, taunting the girls, sometimes flirting with them, beating up kids they didn't like or who looked at them in the wrong way. Then they would go into the town centre and nick mobile phones and purses. With the money they bought designer clothes. Then they would go out partying all night. Tempman was happy. *I was running around doing my ting.*

That's when he first heard of the PDC. One summer evening four boys from Brixton were at the bus station. He was impressed by them. They were older and tougher and had 'names'. They had respect on the streets. Ham, Jigs, Blackshirt and Devious were their tags. Everyone knew they were from the PDC. Tempman too wanted a reputation. He wanted his own name. He got it by targeting other boys – boys who had a bigger name than his.

If other people had a name I took an instant dislike. I'd move to them and beat them up in front of their girlfriend and take money off them.

Even at 15 years old Tempman could be scary. He was big and beefy. But mostly he was scary because he didn't care.

He was now old enough to do what he wanted. He left the foster home in Catford and moved down to his sister's house in Brixton. He didn't let up. He hung around the southern fringes of Angell Town, near Loughborough Junction and Ruskin Park, with Bareman and Snake or Messy and Turfer. Robbing was what they did, street robbing. And some music, MC-ing and rapping. When he woke up in the morning he used to call Messy, Turfer or Devious to meet up with them, to 'link' them.

'What's going on? What are we doing today?'

They never went to school. They just hung around and robbed and got into music. That's when he met Biker and others in the PDC. That's when it went pear-shaped.

It blew up. Everything blew up. Everything. Tempman was always hyperactive. He always had to be doing something. And he always had to be doing that something to extremes.

Suddenly it was times ten. Robbing times ten, girls times ten, drugs times ten, guns times ten.

He criss-crossed south London between Croydon and Brixton. He wanted his name known. He'd get a car and drive around with his friends, his bare torso out of the sunroof. He'd have a 'burner' with him, a gun. He'd head out to places where he knew he could find people he didn't like, people who had a bigger name than him.

He went to every rave, every party, to cause havoc. He wanted to take over. He wanted to be the biggest and baddest 'motherfucker' in south London.

One day in Angell Town he linked up with Biker, Inch's younger brother. Biker wanted to bring him properly into the PDC. Tempman had doubts. He wanted to belong but he wasn't sure whether he wasn't better as a lone operator. With Inch, JaJa and Phat Si in prison it was the younger lot, kids like Biker, Ham and Devious, who were now running things.

We was running everywhere. We was running south London, causing havoc, mashing up tings, robbing tings.

He began to enjoy being in a larger group. They would deal in drugs and rob to buy new clothes and bottles of Hennessey brandy and drink and get high. A hundred of them would jump on a bus and head somewhere in south London to cause more chaos. And Tempman was in charge. It was Biker who'd linked him with the younger PDC.

Biker is my big brudder. He's given me an army. He gave me an army of youngers. I tell you, it was an army.

As the boss of his small army Tempman got to wear Armani, Moschino and Iceberg while the younger kids made do with tracksuits and hoodies. He was someone. He was only 16 but he was now going to raves with the older boys. He sold drugs on the block. His name got round. *Tempman. Tempman. Rah-rah-rah.* He never saved any money. As soon as it came in he would head off to Touchdown in Brixton and buy new trainers and new Armani clothes.

And then the Muslim thing happened. It started slowly at first, with a few of the younger PDC. Muslim was the thing to be. The Taliban, rebellion and Islam were in the air. Muslim preachers were appearing outside the mosques in Stockwell and Brixton. Muslim converts came out of the prisons and started preaching about the Taliban and rebellion and the West's 'demonization' of Islam. In Myatt's Fields estate, on the northern fringe of Angell Town, some of the younger PDC got together and began to boast about being Muslim, about being different from the rest of society, about taking on the West. It was a posture thing. It was a way of scaring people, of getting noticed. Tempman saw it start. Slowly there was a pressure on the streets to convert to Islam.

> *It was a couple of people that were leaders. The rest were followers. That was the effect. Boom. So, boom now, fucking some people were wise enough to think of it differently and do it differently and they would say, you know what, I'd like to pray tomorrow just in case I get shot or run over. Purify themselves of thinking I'm a bad dude. People asked, what is going to happen, what is really going to happen when I die? See what I'm saying? So that's like the way it was. D'you get me G?*

'D'you get me G?' That was Tempman's favourite phrase. 'D'you get me G?' 'G' was short for Gangsta. Tempman's speech mirrored a new harshness on the streets, a harshness that went hand in hand with the new phenomenon that was growing among some of the younger kids – younger kids who robbed and mugged and called themselves Muslims to add to the fear factor. Tempman saw the 'Muslim Boys' phenomenon taking root. He didn't know it but a storm was brewing over the new gang. But just before the storm broke, Tempman was sent to Feltham. He was put inside for driving offences and for assaulting a police officer.

And then it happened. He was in prison when he got the news.

Ham, a PDC guy they all knew and liked, had been shot dead.

The media were saying they knew who was responsible. The newspapers reported that it was a new gang, formed out of the remnants of the PDC, that had shot the 21 year old. They said that the gang was called the 'Muslim Boys' and that they were centred around Myatt's Fields, an estate just to the north of Angell Town. They reported that the 'Muslim Boys' had shot Ham, or Adrian Marriott as he was more properly known, five times in the head, at close range, because he wouldn't convert to Islam.

Chapter Thirty-four

The New Angell Town

You can change the structure. That doesn't make people change. Angell Town will always be Angell Town.

JaJa

It was June when JaJa finally got out of prison and was free to return to Angell Town. It wasn't the first time he'd been back home. For the past three months he'd been on a day-release scheme. Once a month during the weekend he was allowed out of Highpoint prison in Suffolk on a 'town visit'. JaJa would have to give the driving licence and registration number details of either his mum or a PDC friend to the governor and then they would pick him up outside the prison gates at seven in the morning and drive him down the M11 back to Angell Town. He'd spend a few hours at home, eating well, meeting friends or having sex with a girl, before getting in the car and driving back to Suffolk before nightfall.

It was a relief finally to be out. In prison he'd had to suffer the grief of hearing about the killings of Justyn and Ham and the media furore surrounding the Muslim Boys. He'd felt powerless.

Justyn had been one of his best friends. He'd heard about his death one evening when the prison governor called him in.

'Are you all right?'

'Of course I'm all right. Why wouldn't I be?'

'We got a phone call from outside. It was about your…'

JaJa's heart sank. He was sure that the governor was going to say 'your brother'.

He was sure that the governor was going to say that something terrible had happened to Naja.

'It was about your friend, Justyn Morgan. He's been shot. He's dead.'

JaJa was shocked. They'd talked only days before about the future, a bright future. He went numb. All JaJa could think about was the last thing that Justyn had told him.

'Let's get out of this lifestyle and get on with the music.'

This can't go on.

That was what drove JaJa on during his first days out of prison. One of the first things he did when he was out was to go round to Justyn Morgan's house to pay his respects to his grieving family.

He walked into the front room where two of Justyn's uncles were sitting in armchairs, looking tired and defeated. Justyn's mum remained standing looking at JaJa, bewildered.

'You have to stay out of prison. You've got to try and go straight. This must stop.'

JaJa told her about his plans to set up the record label and said that was what he'd always planned to do with Justyn. It had been a project of theirs.

'I'm going to do it, just in the way me and Justyn talked about it.'

That's what set Justyn's mum off. She started crying.

JaJa couldn't help himself. A tear rolled down his own cheek.

'Please don't cry. Please don't cry.'

Justyn's mum told him she was trying to stay strong but that it was hard when she didn't know who the killer of her son was.

'No one is coming forward to give evidence. That's the hardest thing.'

JaJa felt he had to tell her the reality of life on the streets.

'That's how the streets work. It's an eye for an eye.'

Tears streamed down the face of Justyn's mum. JaJa tried to hold it back but even more tears rolled down his cheeks.

For JaJa, the whole drama he'd walked back into was upsetting. He'd lost two friends but he was also annoyed that the blame for the latest killing was being put on a group of kids who were being called the 'Muslim Boys'. He knew the truth was more complicated than a hyped-up story about a group of kids shooting someone because he wouldn't convert to Islam. He knew that feuds in Angell Town were rarely simple. Sometimes they went back years. Sometimes they were to do with money, or a perceived slight, or family. He had heard that Ham had been in an argument with some guys under the railway bridge at Loughborough station just outside Angell Town. A few days later he'd been shot dead. Was it to do with Islam, or was it to do with money? Nobody knew for sure. And nobody would ever really know.

What he did know was that the furore surrounding the 'Muslim Boys' wasn't good for the community. He suspected, rightly as it turned out, that the police had invented the nick-name. JaJa thought it was a police tactic to scare the community and everyone in the justice system. All the police had to do was tell a judge that the accused was associated with the Muslim Boys for the judge to give a harsher sentence. That's what made it so uncomfortable for JaJa when he read articles in the paper linking the PDC with the Muslim Boys.

They put a name on you to make it worse for you. The police came up with that name. That shouldn't be allowed to happen. The police have done it to target people in the streets and if I was in court and someone said I was associated with the 'Muslim Boys', I'd be fucked.

The way JaJa saw the 'Muslim Boys' phenomenon was that there were a few Muslims who had tried to change their lives but who got caught up in a negative lifestyle. The vast majority of the PDC had taken Islam and used it to make their lives better and more disciplined. It was something he understood only too well. He too now considered himself a Muslim.

Many of us have no fathers. We come to Islam for the attachment, for the love. Coz some people have had no love.

He believed there were others, though, a small minority, who got off on the aggressive perception of Islam. They were attracted by the fear that any mention of Osama Bin Laden and the Taliban and terrorism seemed to spread among the population. It was a way of getting attention.

JaJa had seen the growth of Islam from within prison, so

while he was perturbed by the storm over the Muslim Boys he wasn't surprised by it. What did surprise him when he was released were the visible changes to the estate he'd grown up in.

Angell Town had gone through a slow, bureaucratic transformation since the 1990s. JaJa had witnessed the endless public meetings and arguments about how best to regenerate the estate. But during the early years of 2000 real changes had accelerated. Marston House, the council block JaJa grew up in, the place where he had watched the Yardie men and the drug dealers do their business, the place where he too had sold drugs, had been pulled down. New, award-winning housing built from sustainable materials had replaced the old council blocks. Street lighting had gone up. The PDC graffiti had been cleaned off. Walls had been painted with fresh coats of paint. The old concrete football pitch in the centre of the estate had been resurfaced with a smart, new, child-friendly basketball court. A lot had changed.

But there were some things that were still the same. The hairdresser and launderette were still there. So too was the grocer's. And most of the PDC were still there. And while they were all older, deep down they were the same guys he'd grown up with. And JaJa wasn't sure whether that was a good thing or not.

Sharon Kerr wasn't sorry to see the bulldozers in Angell Town. She was glad that Marston House had been pulled down. She had seen too many shootings and stabbings outside her front door. She had been handcuffed too many times during police raids. No, Sharon didn't feel sad when the old council blocks were finally demolished.

My house got raided so many times they called me 'Gangster Mother'. They thought I was the PDC gang leader. They thought I was the ringleader of these boys. I was happy when it came down.

She was moved to a smart, new, terraced house a couple of streets away from Marston House. But in spite of all the redevelopment work she wasn't convinced that Angell Town would be transformed.

I've never seen Angell Town get better. The money they put in did not help. Coz you are always ten years too late. When the thing is happening nobody does anything about it. When it happens everybody makes a hoo-hah about it but nothing changes. People still sell drugs. People still have guns.

And Sharon would be proven right. Angell Town's gun trauma was not over.

Chapter Thirty-five

Pray Days Change

Angell Town. It's changed a lot, but it hasn't changed a lot. You can knock buildings down but the cycle of guns and violence will be still the same.

Inch

It took several weeks for JaJa to regain his bearings. He hadn't been deeply involved with what was going on in Angell Town for so long that it was like reacquainting himself with an old friend. Or perhaps enemy. He spent days checking up on people, looking in on new arrivals who had moved into the estate since he'd last been there.

I'm a people's person – I make sure I know what is happening in my area. Who's that opening a new shop? I'm like that. Who's opening that new pub? Are they Irish? All right, I wanna go there and talk and look around and see what's happening and coz a lot of people have seen me grow up and they know who I am, I know a lot of people.

JaJa had to know what all the different communities that made up Angell Town were getting into. It was intelligence gathering, a way of making sure that he didn't step on other people's toes, but it was also a way of getting information that he could exploit later.

> *Some people do 9 to 5s, some people are doing fraud, some people might be doing other scams like drugs, everyone else might be organizing club nights, or opening shops. Yardies do more drugs and promotions for dances and routines and live stage shows. That's more their kind of thing. The Asian guys – they will open up corner shops and do club nights and drive big BMWs. That's the thing they do, that's their culture thing. The white boys are into everything.*

One of the first places JaJa visited when he got out was the new recording studio that had been fitted out next to the old clubhouse. It had been one of the initiatives that had emerged out of Dora Boatemah's campaign to regenerate the estate. Dora had died a few years before, but her former partner, Earl Myers, kept the keys to the studio and made sure that it ran smoothly.

Earl had started the studio project in the early 1990s when it was nothing more than a boxroom in a corner of one of the empty flats in Marston House, just down the corridor from where JaJa lived. The aim was to give the youth from the estate something to do. To begin with it was no more than a tape deck and a desk. But, as government and council money came in, the studio was moved to one of the old burnt-out garages beneath Fairfax

House where it was sound-proofed, carpeted and kitted out with new electronics. It was where acts like Blak Twang, Roots Manuva and Ty, who years later would top the hip-hop charts, developed their sound.

When JaJa came calling it created a dilemma for Earl. He had always been into more cultured music, a mellow reggae that put out a message of peace and love, like in the old days. He'd even stuck homemade posters on the walls of the studio in an attempt to get his philosophy across to those who used the facilities.

Put down the ill, ill, ill,
Learn to build, build, build.

Greater Unity.

The trouble was that the music had changed from the old-style dancehall sound systems that used to be strung together in Angell Town. What was now blasting out on the streets of Angell Town was heavy, hardcore music from Jamaica, 'bad boy tunes' with hardcore lyrics that went on about 'smoking the feds' and 'I've got my gun and I'm not afraid to blast you'. Earl feared that lyrics about 'killer men' and 'road thugs' only served to glorify and glamorize gangs and guns.

That kinda flipped my brain for a while. I wanted to get
positivity in the community and all I was hearing was 'kill
this', 'murder that', this is what I'm saying. And it wasn't
just kids. Adults were doing it. To tell the truth it sapped
my energy.

He'd seen a new coldness on the streets that he didn't like. Even though he had lived on the estate for much of his life and was a big man who no one would really want to mess with, he felt that a wrong look at the wrong time would end in trouble.

He didn't like the new rapping about cop killers and guns and gangs but in spite of this he knew he'd have to give JaJa a chance. He couldn't control everything that people did on the estate. For £10 an hour he hired the studio out to JaJa and others in the PDC and let JaJa do his thing.

JaJa didn't recognize Earl's worries. He was out of prison, had big plans and he needed money to make it happen. He had one ambition now.

We're gonna get the whole PDC thing rocking.

And 'to get the PDC rocking' they needed to 'tax' people.

Some of the PDC went up to some of the local drug dealers.

'You know what we're about. You need to pay a contribution.'

They called it a 'tax'. Others might call it extortion, protection money.

Even though he had spent so many years in prison, everyone on the estate knew who JaJa was and they knew he could be nasty. They knew that he had the power to shut down their drug-dealing operations.

They know what sort of person I am. They know about my reputation. They know about the PDC. That's why they will decide to be nice and pay up.

Within weeks of JaJa's release some of the PDC had collected 'tax' money. The talk was of what the PDC were going to do. And the talk was big. They got hold of 4,000 blank CDs and cases, rented out the Angell Town recording studio for days at a time and began to put down some tracks that JaJa and others in the PDC had written. Not all of the PDC could 'spit', as rapping was called, but it didn't matter. New people came out of prison and swelled the PDC ranks.

It was a hot summer. Everyone got caught up in a frenzy of music, money and violence. There were more shootings. More media stories about the Muslim Boys. As the summer got hotter, there was no let-up to the violence or the madness. Every day there was something happening. For some of the younger members like Tempman it was a real adventure. Someone came out of prison, the robbing continued, someone got shot but the music kept coming. And JaJa pressed on with cutting the PDC's first album.

The CD was ready in September 2004. It was called *Pray Days Change*. Some of the younger kids from Angell Town were sent out onto the streets with boxes of CDs and they got a small commission for each CD they sold. There were forty tracks with names like 'Da Streets', 'Gangsta, Gangsta' and 'PDC 4 Life'. The raps explored the frustration and the posturing of street life. All the PDC contributed. They all wrote some of the lyrics. One of the tracks, 'Fallen Soldiers', was dedicated to Justyn Morgan and all their friends who'd been shot dead on the streets of Angell Town. The CD was punctuated with the simulated sound of pistol and machine-gun fire.

It was when the DVD came out that trouble started once again.

It was JaJa who arranged for the video to be made. He

contacted some cameramen he knew, from an outfit called Streetz Incarcerated. JaJa didn't know what he was doing but it didn't matter. He always seemed to have links to the right people and faith that it would all come off. The cameramen just turned up one day. JaJa and fifty members of the PDC found a wall in Angell Town and began filming. He'd never done a video before but it seemed to work. JaJa, Inch, Tempman and Ribz were all there, rapping and posturing in their New York Yankee baseball caps, Nike shoes and designer jackets. Inch and JaJa rapped about the friends they'd lost to gunfire and gangs, about Justyn Morgan being shot in the chest. As he rapped, Inch fired an imaginary gun.

The video got some airplay on the U Video channel on Sky. The word on the streets was that the video was good. In Brixton and Angell Town it was the hottest thing. *They're mad for it. They're going nuts.*

Then the storm arrived. The police objected. They said it contained too many references to gangs and guns. They said it glorified violence. It was true the video was full of shocking lyrics about guns and gangs but for many it was just harmless posturing. The satellite channel listened to the advice of the police, pulled the video and blacklisted the PDC. JaJa felt he knew what was going on. But he wasn't bitter. It was the best time of his life. It was a long time since he had been happy. But the day the video got some airplay he was probably the happiest he'd ever been.

Earl Myers took a backseat. He didn't like what was going on. He didn't like all the hype about violence and guns. He didn't think that that was the role of music. He wished that the vibe in the studio in Angell Town was different.

Trying to talk to young people about that today, forget it.
It's like talking to a herd of stampeding elephants. You can't
do it. You're gonna get crushed. Especially if you are talking
to a group. As individuals you get a better response.
Somebody's got a front coz he's with his crew. Usually the
one who is fronting ain't the one who is really doing it. It's
hangers-on from the entourage. A lot of people get caught in
the fashion thing so, coz your friend is doing it, you partake.

He had to hold back his objections when *bad men with attitude* walked into his studio. They were big, dangerous men who were all swagger and snarls, people who didn't say 'nuttin' to nobody'. He saw them controlling the hangers-on through intimidation and violence. He saw the hold they had on the younger ones just through the way they used to bully them. That's when he understood the power of gangs and crews.

It was 90 per cent hardcore attitude. You could hear it
burning through their voices, their aggressive voices. Their
voices were burning with attitude.

But he was in for a surprise.

He pressed ahead and decided to ignore the posturing and the fronting and let go of his prejudices.

I thought, I'd gotta work with what I gotta work with.
Work with what you got. This is like a filter. Bad attitude

walks through the door but by the time they go out, or a
couple of sessions later, it's a lot better.

He had never expected it. Hard men who were linked to the
PDC came in and didn't even acknowledge him. They sat down
in the studio smoking weed, their feet on the table, growling and
snarling amongst each other. But a couple of sessions later, once
they'd laid down their tracks, they were changed men. As they
left the Angell Town studio, they waved a hand at Earl and
smiled at him.

'Thanks, Earl. Bless.'

It restored some of Earl's faith in the redemptive power of
music and the good that he and his studio were doing for the
community. He began to see what JaJa was hoping to achieve
through the PDC and their music. The 'Greater Unity' posters
he'd put up on the studio wall weren't so out of touch after all.

If you're not prepared to do nuttin' or offer a kind word of
encouragement to people, forget talking, do something
about it. We all can't be at the frontline but as long as you
are contributing you can talk but if you ain't contributing,
don't talk to me … But boy, it's been hard on my head.

As the summer gave way to winter, police rounded up three men
for the murder of Adrian Marriott – Ham. One of them was carrying a loaded handgun when he was arrested outside a mosque
in Croydon. A triumphant story about the arrest of the leader-
ship of the 'Muslim Boys' was splashed all over the south London papers. Police thought they had cracked the case. But

nobody would talk in court. The murder trial collapsed through lack of evidence.

The violence continued. Blacker came out of prison, followed soon after by Phat Si. Phat Si threw himself straight into the frenzy over the PDC. The hype over *Pray Days Change* drew him in. He didn't want to get involved in violence but violence followed Phat Si wherever he went.

A few weeks after he was out of prison, violence followed Phat Si to the heart of Angell Town, to the streets right outside JaJa's house.

Chapter Thirty-six

The Shootout

It was the first time I'd been there when a friend got shot. It was made right there, bruv. Secretly I was scared. D'you get me G? You didn't know who they were going to shoot.

Tempman

Tempman believed the shooting could have been prevented. It was a feud that went back some way. It could have been about drugs, or family, or respect. No one was quite telling. There were some things that were better left unsaid. But it was a feud that Tempman believed should have ended differently.

Phat Si had always been hyperactive. He'd always got into more trouble than the others. And that night, as the excitement over the *Pray Days Change* album escalated, a small group had gathered in the street outside JaJa's house.

Tempman was with three friends. Four metres away, facing them, like some gunslingers shootout in a cowboy film,

244

was the man they'd been arguing with and two of his friends. Some of them had 'straps' or guns. There was a moment when it was clear to Tempman that the dispute would escalate into violence.

Them men got their ting, my man has got his ting. They got their strap. It was like a showdown and I'm standing there with no gun. And Phat Si was there shouting and hollering and it was like boom, boom, boom and all of a sudden Phat Si got hit. D'you get me G? I blowed back. I ran away. Somebody called the ambulance.

Phat Si was on the floor. His shouts echoed round Angell Town.

'My leg! They shot my leg.'

He curled up on the floor screaming until the ambulance came.

Like many of the shootings in Angell Town, no one talked. The police never got to the bottom of what happened.

A few days after that Angell Town was rocked by yet more violence. This time it was a murder.

Chapter Thirty-seven

The Shooting of Blacker

People can get shot for any reason. You can get shot for
fucking someone's sister. You can get shot in the head and
you don't know why. Your story's finished. That's real life.

Inch

JaJa was on his new Suzuki GSX R600. Why shouldn't he have
a brand new motorbike? He was out of prison and he wanted
something to show for it. The trouble was it made him more
noticeable. That night was no exception. It was the last few days
of 2004. He was on his way to a radio station to promote the *Pray
Days Change* DVD. He was speeding through south London.
And the police were chasing him.

It wasn't unusual. All the PDC had been involved in chases
with the police. Sometimes the police got them. Other times they
managed to get away. This time JaJa didn't get away.

He was accelerating through West Norwood, with the police
on his tail. They were right on him. He was thinking that if he
could just get round the next corner he might escape. He was

buzzing with adrenaline. He'd been buzzing with adrenaline for months now. He turned the corner and…

Sharon Kerr was at home when she got the call. It was Birdie.

'Elijah's been knocked off his bike. The police are here.'

She loaded Naja and the girls in the car and drove to the scene.

When she got to West Norwood, she saw her son lying on the road, his limbs at different angles, his bike totally smashed up. He was unconscious. Police had cordoned off the scene. At that stage she didn't know why, but the police were being unusually attentive, calling her by her first name, acting, she thought, as though they were concerned. She saw Inch standing around just outside the police cordon. She saw him trying to attract her attention. He was winking at her. She knew what it meant. JaJa might have things on him that he wasn't supposed to have. Sharon did what she was supposed to do. It was routine for her. *This is how I help Elijah and I always will.*

She'd watched enough TV to know what to do next. She started wailing and crying, and pushed her way through the police cordon to her son. *It was an act, all that crying. I'm not like that because I'm hardened to it all.* Inch again signalled to her. If JaJa had something on him that he shouldn't have, she could take it off him. She padded him down. He was 'clear'. The ambulance men stretchered her son into the ambulance and Sharon followed. Inch was still signalling to her. She went through his pockets again to make sure that he had nothing on him.

Lying in the road, unseen by everyone, was something that looked very much like an ammunition clip.

JaJa was out for hours. Sharon feared he might be dead. She stared at the plastic 'Resuscitation' sign written on the door of the room where JaJa was being treated and came to a decision, a decision that she'd come to many, many times before.

> *If he survives this I'm not doing this no more. I've finished.*
> *He's of age and he's got to stop doing it because I've done*
> *loads of things for Elijah. Loads. Loads of things. I've*
> *covered for him. And I don't mean to.*

She didn't want to be standing there again in a few weeks time with all his friends looking at her as if to ask 'Is he clean?' No, she didn't want to do it again. She didn't want to go through her act to sort him out any more.

When he came round the first thing she did was reassure him that he was clean.

'Everything is safe.'

He closed his eyes again. She would help him financially, but she wouldn't cover for him any more. She'd decided. Enough was enough. No more.

'I'm not having it. You've got to do it on your own. Whatever problem you get into you've got to do it on your own. I'm fed up.'

She couldn't tell if he was listening.

'I'm not going to help you any more. If you get into trouble with the police again you are on your own.'

She sat staring at her motionless son, telling herself over and over again that she had made her decision. She wouldn't help him out any more. She wouldn't cover for him no more. That was it. From now on, he was on his own.

It was only later Sharon discovered why the police had been

acting so concerned. It was a police car that had knocked her son off his bike. That's why the main charges against JaJa were dropped. The police decided to take no further action.

JaJa woke up in hospital a day later with a snapped elbow, bruised pelvis and several metal pins holding his arms together.

'You were a very lucky young man.'

That's all the doctors would tell him. He was still in hospital on New Year's Eve 2004 when the shooting happened.

It was 7 p.m. and the New Year's Eve parties were gearing up in Angell Town. A few miles away in Thornton Heath, a silver Renault Clio was cruising the streets. Suddenly out of nowhere came the sound of gunshots. Bullets peppered the doors and windows of the car from several angles. There were three men inside the car. The one sitting in the back seat was hit in the chest and head. As Big Ben rang in the New Year, news filtered through to Angell Town that one of the car's occupants had just died in hospital. It was Blacker, the street name for JaJa's and Inch's PDC friend, Solomon Martin.

Inch first knew that something was up when his phone wouldn't stop ringing. Finally he answered it.

'Blacker's dead.'

Inch went silent.

'They're saying you and JaJa did it.'

'Don't be stupid.'

But Inch was worried. He and JaJa were friends with

Blacker but they'd had a falling out several weeks before and everybody knew it.

His phone rang again.

'Blacker's been shot.'

'I know.'

Inch knew he hadn't been involved but he knew that things could be blown out of proportion, that people would talk. It was always madness in Angell Town.

JaJa was still in hospital when he heard about the murder. He was upset and angry. Then he was worried. Then he was relieved.

If I was on the road, if I was out, I would have went to prison because everyone thought it was me. It was like a saviour, me having a crash. For a fact I know that if I didn't have that bike crash I would have been in jail for that. Definitely, for murder.

In the eyes of some, JaJa was a prime suspect. It related to an ongoing dispute in Angell Town. A dispute involving Blacker and others in the PDC.

Me and him were best friends. The argument wasn't between me and Blacker. When Blacker died everyone thought, 'It must be Elijah that done it, it must be a revenge thing.' That's why I got blamed for it. Because it happened so quickly, not everyone knew about the bike crash and then Blacker got shot a couple of days later. It didn't sink in to everyone that I was in hospital and that I couldn't have done it.

Inch expected that there would be a knock on the door at any moment.

I thought I was going to be nicked and my fear was that the police would come round and put me on remand just because people said I done it. They were buying into the Inch and Elijah factor. They think we are together. I was pissed and I couldn't think about what I was supposed to think about because everyone was on my dick. It was the lowest point in my life.

It annoyed him that people on the estate immediately thought the two of them were the cause of the trouble. Yes, Blacker and JaJa had had a dispute. But neither JaJa nor Inch would kill him. They were friends with Blacker. They were friends with Li'l Shak, Blacker's brother. He felt angry and confused. He hoped the police would quickly find out who did it. But life in Angell Town was rife with intrigue and gossip and retribution. None of the rivalries were very clear. Sometimes two crews would be rivals just because something stupid had been said or done. And Inch knew that it could lead to retaliation and resentments that lasted for years.

Sometimes though, in Angell Town, you didn't even need a look or a word. Sometimes there was no reason. It was as simple as that.

He had been shot at a couple of times. Both times were outside a club. And he never knew why.

You can be shot at and it's just because you are in the wrong place at the wrong time. I might get shot right now, vrooom, vrooom, and I wouldn't have an inkling of who did it and why.

Sharon Kerr was at home when JaJa called her from hospital.

'Don't go out. If someone knocks on the door, make sure you know who it is first.'

Over the next few days, she heard rumours on the street that there was a vendetta against them. She heard that Solomon's family were out to kill JaJa or one of his family. Sharon wondered how it had got to this. She had always treated Solomon like her own son. He used to stay with them at Marston House when they were kids. Sharon's cousin had a baby with him. It was family but it was messed-up family.

We've lived a pretty scary life now that I'm talking about it. It was scary that Christmas because Elijah was in hospital and we thought he was dying and there were death threats against us because of Solomon's murder. And because Elijah wasn't around, more rumours started to spread and people were out to kill us. Family. Everybody has to live a certain way, innit? And if someone does something out of that way it's either coz they messed up or they weren't thinking straight and were not thinking about another brother.

The trouble was that family feuds, like feuds on the street, ran deep. Sharon believed that it was impossible to apologize within the community. Once something had been done, it was impossible to undo it. It was months before relations between the two families were cleared up and Sharon felt she could breathe easier. *They still don't know who killed Solomon, but they now know it's not us.*

JaJa's sister Chantelle wasn't sure whether anyone would ever know who did it. In the end, to stay alive, everyone in the community had to keep their mouths shut.

And with no one talking, the police were unable to make progress in finding out who murdered Solomon Martin.

In hospital, JaJa began to think more deeply about his situation. He'd seen three of his friends die in the space of a few months. What was it that had made these things happen? He wanted to know whose fault it was. Was it something in him? Was it the friends he hung around? Was it Angell Town? Was there a way out of the cycle of violence?

> *There are always those in Angell Town who won't like me. On the street, say I had a fight in the park all those years ago, someone I'd stabbed or punched, and he has never liked me, at every chance he badmouths me and will always have a go at me. So we are rivals and we group up as rivals. So when that same man sees us on the DVDs then they hate us even more. Either way they are still talking about me. There are always people who hate you in Angell Town.*

He didn't mind admitting that he was scared. *When is it going to stop? I might be next.* Instead of slowing him down though it gave him more determination to push ahead, to go on and do better things to get out of the vicious circle. *The madness can't continue. The madness mustn't continue.*

Chapter Thirty-eight

The Business

*Music's a lot of things that breaks the way and you know
that Americans set the trend because the biggest role models
we look up to are the 50 cents, the Jay Zs. And you know
what? Badness or sex sells because anyone who's talking
reality doesn't really sell so when you're talkin' your life
whether it's badness, sex or whatever that's selling. That's
making people 100s of millions.*

Bloods

JaJa knew he wouldn't be able to start PDC as a proper business
if there were gunfights and police chases at night, if people
inside and outside the estate were scared of the crew members.
He knew he had to get individual PDC members to commit to
being part of the business. He asked each of them to put £1,500
into a pot to rent an office. Then he told them that if they were
going to be serious they would have to settle down. *We have to be
more business-like, more entertainment friendly.* The first move
was to adjust the name. Instead of Peel Dem Crew, JaJa wanted

something that would sound more positive and make a point. That's when he came up with Poverty Driven Children. *Poverty drove us to crime.* Devious came up with a rap line they all liked.

'We're poverty driven, we're driven by poverty.'

JaJa didn't like the word 'gang'. It seemed a naïve way of describing how he saw the PDC. He saw it as 'a crew', a loose affiliation of young black men like himself, almost like an umbrella organization. First there were five of them, then ten, then twenty. And it just kept expanding. He didn't like the way the 'gangs' were described in the media. He didn't like the way the media made out that they were some sort of amateurish band of thugs. He saw the word 'gang' being used by the media as a way to sell their newspaper stories and their TV documentaries. For JaJa the PDC was much more sophisticated and complicated than that. They would work freelance, but they also helped each other out. They had robbed, mugged and dealt in drugs but they also tried to do their music events and their rapping. It was a social network, a way of regaining some power, and the more people the word went out to, the better.

To calm things down he persuaded individuals within the PDC to kick back for a while. After a studio session, he suggested to members of the crew that they go straight home rather than congregate outside the studio. Some, though, found the lure of the streets more difficult to resist than others.

Tempman had never been one of those who found it easy to stay at home. Ever since he was six or seven years old he'd spent his time living on the streets. And that's where all his friends were to be found. At night some of those associated with the 'Muslim

Boys' came calling and told him to forget about the music and go out on the road with them.

> *I was 100 per cent with music and everything. It's what I know, innit? I was with the PDC but my brudders what were still Muslim used to come around, yeah kind of thing, they came round trying to pull me back. I was chillin', I'm back on the PDC and still praying. It was all right. We was getting airplay, mix tapes were coming out, it was PDC mad. Do you get me G? We used to drive around, go smoke and give out CDs.*

Birdie was smart. As the PDC music took off he was able to take it all in his stride. He'd still managed to stay out of prison, unlike all his friends. The closest he'd come was a few years before when he let his mate Asher drive his car. He was driving erratically and the police stopped them. Birdie had drugs in the car and as they pulled over he tried to throw the packets out of the window. But the police saw it and he got taken to the station and charged with possession of a class A drug. He was fined £150 and that was it.

He'd taken to the music slowly at first. He knew nothing about making beats and setting up music equipment but he would sit in the recording studio in Angell Town, watching and listening. When the studio was emptied of the main players he would get in there and, with the encouragement of Earl Myers, he learned patiently how the equipment worked and how to mix tapes.

It wasn't long before he was up to speed and others in the PDC began to look to him to work the studio computer and create their sound. He saw himself as the producer. He didn't care so much about rapping. He didn't want to be rapping at 35 years old. He wanted to make beats. He wanted to create a unique sound that would sell.

We want to get the name out there. We want to get it pumping. We want PDC to be a name you recognize. Part of PDC is that we don't want to be classed under 'Urban'. We want to be classed as street music.

He was knowledgeable about music and it made him mad that the music industry linked all black music together under the title 'Urban'.

Blazin' Squad is new grime music. Bob Marley is classic reggae. Don't they see that Blazin' Squad has a different sound to Bob Marley?

Not everyone was as patient and thorough as Birdie. JaJa was in a hurry. He knew that time wasn't on his side. He was under pressure from people, particularly the younger kids, who were looking up to him and who wanted to see some real results. He knew that unless the PDC had some success soon, the younger kids would get bored and start causing problems just as he had done when he'd been younger.

If I take too long the young kids go hungry and cause a lot of shit all over again, that's why everyone is looking up to me, to bring more stuff into the 'hood.

JaJa knew that it was his fault. He had got expectations going. He had got everyone's hopes up. *I've got to be man enough now to take it on.*

What he didn't realize was that one of the things he had to sort out was another media storm about the PDC and their links to gun crime.

Chapter Thirty-nine

Murder, Murder, murder. Death, Death, Death.

The newspapers don't put the real stuff out. They don't ask us really what happens. They just find one of their like, one of their co-workers, sons or something, put him in the paper with a couple of knives posing and that so they can sell copies and go, 'Yeah, it's a bad gang, the PDC.'

Bloods

In the first half of 2005, the people of Brixton and in particular Angell Town were still reeling from the aftershock of Solomon Martin's murder. Solomon was the son of Steve Martin, better known as Blacker Dread, a respected musician and producer whose record store on Coldharbour Lane was a Brixton institution. The community joined together in grief. Anti-gun rallies were organized with impassioned pleas from local politicians and celebrities that the violence had to stop.

But it didn't. There were more newspaper reports of gun violence by the 'Muslim Boys'. New gun crime statistics pointed to yet another rise in firearms offences.

Once again, the PDC found themselves back in the news. And Tempman was at the centre of the controversy.

One evening during the summer, a video of the PDC rapping appeared first on the local, then on the national news.

Tempman was shown rapping in an extract from a mix tape called *Game Over*.

'Murder, murder, murder, death, death, death.'

That's all they showed. And the news played it over and over again.

In another DVD for Sticky Businezz, Tempman rapped about life on the streets on a track called 'Round Ere'. As he rapped, those around him made gun-firing motions with their hands.

When I see a constable, I'm not comfortable
That 38 won't save you
When I see a fed man, he's a dead man.

Sharon Kerr was at home when she saw her son, JaJa, appear on an item about gang violence on the *Ten O'Clock News*. According to the news report he was gloating about being the boss of the PDC. She was glad his grandmother wasn't around to see it.

If my mum ever saw that she'd have a heart attack. I'm happy my mum was in Jamaica.

Bloods was in Maidstone prison watching the news when he saw his PDC 'brothers' paraded on a television report about gangs and gun terror.

Like my brothers are terrorists and I'm seeing them say my brothers are terrorists. What terrorists? We weren't doing no terrorists. We are trying to go forward. We take one step forward and they're pushing us two steps back.

Pod, one of the guys who had been in the 28s and who had known JaJa since he was a kid, also followed the media story with disgust. He was now a respected Christian preacher and gospel singer and father to four kids. He had been impressed by JaJa's efforts with the PDC and felt that the story was being twisted to make them look bad.

I thought the PDC was coming into positiveness by going into music and coming off the streets. I thought that was a positive move that they made. To see Inch and Elijah taking up the microphone to rap about their lifestyle and what's going on by explaining street life, was a good thing.

He didn't even mind that JaJa had converted to Islam. Pod tried to advise him about his life and talked to him about becoming a Christian and going to church. JaJa would always listen patiently and explain why he had chosen to become a Muslim and why he felt he had to lead a lifestyle that centred around the streets, the PDC and their music.

> *One thing about Elijah, he respected certain people and if he
> thought they were positive and they had something going on
> in their lives he would be friendly. I thought if you are going
> to be a Muslim then be a Muslim. Better to know
> themselves through Islam than to be ignorant.*

JaJa kept his head down and waited for the guns and gangs
storm that was swirling around the PDC to die away. Except it
didn't. It was about to strike at the very centre of their world.

Chapter Forty

Shot in the Head

We just want to climb now. We don't want no more negative stuff. We just want positive. More positive equals more positive, do you get me? We're fed up with negativity. Twenty-five years of negativity ain't good. See what I'm saying? Trust me, we need progress now. No one don't like living in squalor and everyone likes to live comfortable, innit? I want a piece of the cake as well, and my brothers. We want in.

Phat Si

It took some time for Phat Si to adjust to life on the outside. It had been a mad few months. He'd come out of prison to the hype about the video for 'Fallen Soldiers' and had fallen into the excitement with glee. He'd been shot in the leg. But in the midst of the chaos he was also trying to get some stability back into his life. He still smoked weed, lots of it, and most nights he could be found at the Angell Town studio with Bloods and the others slowly getting off his head.

'You're mashing yourself up.'

That's what JaJa had told him more than once.

For his part, JaJa could see that some of the PDC smoked too much weed, that they were getting dopey. From the outside looking in, it was clear. *I tell them but they don't see it*. He didn't like it when they were off their heads and he told them so.

'This is not fun any more.'

But none of them would listen. They carried on puffing away.

Except Ribz. He stopped smoking and drinking because he knew it was messing him up and because Islam had now become an important anchor in his life. It was what stabilized him. He started going to the gym and lifting weights. He had always been skinny. That's how he'd got his street name. But now he began putting on bulk. In the space of a few months he shot up from 9 stone to 18 stone. Soon it was the gym that became an addiction. He drank protein milkshakes every day and because he'd stopped smoking weed he had a permanent attack of the munchies. He ate and ate and ballooned. Even the gym work couldn't keep his weight down. One day he was in bed and could hardly breathe because of the weight on his chest. He woke up spluttering with his belly wobbling uncomfortably. That's when he knew he had to change his whole lifestyle and cut down on his visits to the gym, and the fridge.

Fuck it! I'm gonna chill for a bit and get rid of this weight.

To discipline himself he turned again to Islam.

Phat Si never got religion. Islam didn't get to him in the way that it did to some of the others.

When someone's eyes are opened to religion there's nothing like it.

But Phat Si never saw the light.

Since he'd left Canada six years earlier he'd never seen his son. And he hadn't seen Lisa, the mother of his son, either. He had no idea where they were. He'd asked his mother, his sisters, his cousins who still lived in Toronto, but no one knew. He thought back to when he was happiest. It was when his mum and dad were still together when he was six or seven. *It's been pear-shaped ever since.*

What haunted him and made him angry was the thought that he had suffered a lifetime of betrayal. He had been let down by those around him. What had kept him sane over the years was not parents, or family, or neighbours, or girlfriends. It was the guys from the PDC who had remained true.

And the thing I reckon that brought us closer together is the fact of having snakes around, innit? Like you grow up with people and they're not really what you think they are so you see the real ones and you stick to them, innit? And the real ones will stick to you more as well, innit? You don't really want no fake people round.

But there was hope for the future. There was hope because he wanted wealth, health and happiness for himself and for his friends. He was expecting a baby with his new girlfriend. *The future's gonna be bright and beautiful.*

Phat Si got shot on Sunday 15 October 2006. He was with Skippy and Tiny. They'd gone to a club in Elephant and Castle to buy some weed. It was a Jamaican music night where they were playing ragga music. Even though Phat Si preferred funky house and garage he'd gone there anyway. That's where the guy had arranged for him to pick up the weed. It was 3.30 a.m. Suddenly there was an argument inside the club. Shots rang out. Skippy, Tiny and Phat Si ran out into the street.

Skippy ran one way, Tiny ran another. Phat Si ran past the Ministry of Salsa on Walworth Road. More shouting. More shots. One shot ricocheted off a car and hit a bystander in the leg. Another shot rang out. The bullet hit Phat Si in the head.

It was 3.35 in the morning and Inch was waiting for Phat Si. He was in Southend, at a rave. He wasn't worried that Phat Si hadn't turned up yet. Phat Si's timing was erratic at the best of times. And anyway he'd spoken to him a few hours earlier, at around midnight.

'I'm on my way soon. I'm waiting on Tiny.'

Inch had persuaded Phat Si to help him promote a rave that night in Southend. They'd been together at the same venue the previous week. It had been a hectic night because Inch and Tiny had got involved in a fight with some locals. No one knew how it started. One moment Inch had been paying the DJ, the next moment someone had thrown a punch and all hell had broken loose. Phat Si had been on his way back to the club with some Rizla papers he'd just bought. He'd missed the whole thing. He was angry that by the time he got back the fight had been broken up and the warring parties separated. Phat Si felt that he'd missed out. That's why he was happy to agree to go back to the same rave the following Saturday.

On Saturday 14 October, Inch had got to the venue early to

help prepare the place and the sound system. He'd had a discussion with Phat Si, who told him that he would make his own way there.

Just after midnight he had the conversation with Phat Si in which he said he'd be on his way as soon as he'd picked up Tiny.

An hour later Inch got a call from two girls who said they were waiting on Phat Si to drive them to the Southend rave.

'We've been waiting for ages. He hasn't turned up yet.'

Inch wasn't that bothered. He knew he was probably picking up some weed from somewhere and would be there soon. Phat Si drove fast and could do the journey in around an hour.

It was now four in the morning. Inch had just stepped out to get some cigarette papers from an all-night shop. When he got back a friend told him he'd missed a call. Someone called Bloods was trying to get hold of him. He was to call him back as soon as possible.

It was urgent.

He dialled Bloods's number.

'Phat Si's dead, you know.'

Bloods spoke with such calm that Inch didn't really understand what was going on.

'What do you mean? What are you saying?'

'Phat Si got shot, man. He's dead.'

Inch went into shock.

'What are you talking about?'

'Someone's just called me. He's right there. Phat Si is dead on the ground. He's laying there. He's dead.'

Inch went into meltdown. He started crying right then and there.

He tried to call everyone's phone number to find out what was going on. But everybody was engaged. He tried to call Bloods back to find out who he'd heard the news from. He wanted to speak directly to someone who knew what was going on. Bloods's phone was engaged.

He flew into a panic. He felt he was going nuts.

'Where's JaJa? Where's Tiny?'

Then all of a sudden his phone started ringing again.

It was just after four in the morning when JaJa got a call.

'Where are you?'

'I'm in bed.'

'Someone's been shot in Elephant and Castle and they say it was someone in the PDC. I just wanted to make sure you were all right.'

'No, man, I'm fine.'

The phone rang again. It was someone else who was checking up on him.

'Are you all right. Did you get shot?'

'No, I'm in my house.'

Whenever there's a shooting everyone thinks it's me. I get shot, kidnapped, I get everything every day. Anything happens, they think it's me. The rumours are I get shot in my head on Friday, shot in my leg on Saturday, and let out of jail on Sunday. There are so many rumours on the road.

Then Skippy phoned.

'Phat Si got shot. He was lying on the floor. I think he's dead.'

JaJa didn't know what to think. He rang his fellow PDC crew, Li'l Shak and Maddix. They came round straightaway in the car. Then they drove straight to King's College Hospital in Denmark Hill and met up with Ribz who had also heard the news.

The police were waiting for them.

'Get down on the floor. Take out your guns.'

They lay down on the floor and got searched. JaJa knew what was going on. *They thought we were coming to finish him off, innit?* From the adrenaline and pumped-up tone of their voices JaJa suspected that the police were enjoying the drama of investigating a suspected gang shooting. He thought they were getting off on the power.

Skippy, pale and silent, was in the waiting room with Phat Si's girlfriend.

A nurse walked by and looked in on them and gestured to the ward.

'This one is a gonner.'

Then another nurse walked by.

'If he pulls through, he'll be paralysed for life.'

The news kept changing every hour. First he was dead, then he wasn't dead.

When JaJa and the others were allowed in to see him they were met with a shocking sight. Phat Si was lying there, eyes closed, pale and drawn, attached to a tangle of liquid-filled tubes. The worst sight was his head, swollen and misshapen under layers of bloody bandages.

It was hours before JaJa managed to make some sort of sense of what he was seeing.

I've come to the stage when I'm used to it. I've lost loads of my friends. Because he was my friend I was pissed. But obviously it wasn't that big a wow factor. I looked at him and think OK, that's what I'm saying. That's what we're living through. That's what happens if you're out there, if you're out and about not being careful. That's what happens. He knows that as well.

Inch reacted in a different way. He felt tears rising up when he saw his friend lying there. His heart beat faster. He felt sick to his stomach.

It was hurtful. I felt like it was me laying there, innit? I was feeling it.

They all knew that Phat Si had been through a lot in his life. He'd been shot and stabbed, arrested, beaten up, on the run. He'd done everything. He always seemed to get mixed up in some madness. Now, though, they had to come to terms with the fact that he might die. No one wanted to dwell on it too much. For JaJa there was no point in just standing there in the hospital staring at him day after day. He went home and for the next few weeks he used to call up Phat Si's girl to check up on him. For a long time it was touch and go. But when news came, it was good news.

The word came down the grapevine that Phat Si had moved an arm. Then he moved a leg. The nurses were surprised. But still they couldn't see him as anything other than 'a walking dead man'.

When they finally moved Phat Si to a normal ward JaJa went to see him again. Phat Si smiled and tried to speak, but no words came out. Just vague noises.

Doctors explained that he was paralysed down one side of his body and that he could understand but might never be able to walk or talk properly again.

JaJa found it hard to look at him. His friend had been so vibrant, so powerful. Now he had a huge lump on the side of his head and his normally expressive face was pale and skinny. He couldn't talk and instead would make only vague watery noises that JaJa couldn't decipher. JaJa had no idea what the future might hold for Phat Si. The doctors had decided it was too dangerous to extract the bullet, so they left it there, lodged in the side of his head.

The news about Phat Si spread beyond Angell Town. He'd been such a central character in the life of the estate over the previous twenty years that everybody, even those who had moved on, wanted to know what had happened. When the rumours reached Pod, who was now working as a pastor in Croydon, he was shocked. But he wasn't surprised. Pod had seen Phat Si's life unfold before his eyes. Ever since Phat Si had stabbed him in the leg when Si was just 11 years old he thought he knew how it would go. Pod knew only too well what happened to those who spent their life around guns and drugs. He'd watched as, one by one, several of his contemporaries in the 28s had lost their lives on the streets of south-west London.

Keith Weed, one of the original 28s, had been stabbed in an attack by a white gang near Kennington. Sykes had been shot dead in Brixton. Duffers, who he'd gone to school with, had been shot dead during a stupid argument at a local party. Hustler, the 28 who they all looked up to when they were kids, was one of the few who was still alive, living a chilled life in Brixton with his family.

No, Pod wasn't surprised by what happened to Phat Si. He'd known too many people who had died because of the wrong look, or because they'd stolen something from the wrong person, or from some other stupidity.

You could see how Si's life was going from a young age. He could have taken someone's life and gone to prison. That's how his destiny was. That's how his journey turned out.

It was because of what had happened to so many of the 28s that he made an effort to stay in contact with some of the surviving members of the gang. He often tried to get them to church. Not many of them ever accepted. But a few months earlier he'd asked some of them to come to his brother's wedding. His brother's wife-to-be had stood up and sung 'I will always love you' at the ceremony. Some of the toughest, baddest guys in the 28s ended up in tears in the church. To Pod, that was a powerful reminder of the bond that still linked them together.

It goes to show that there is still happiness on the street. It's not all bad. We still call each other 'cus', for cousin, even though we are not strictly family. But that's the point. We are still a family.

That's why he had so much faith in JaJa and what he was doing with the PDC. He believed that the PDC guys had now grown up and were a good, not a malign influence on the streets. He knew how powerfully the streets spoke. When he was young he had been influenced by the older boys. He had seen how he and the rest of the 28s had influenced JaJa and the Younger 28s. Now he saw the influence the PDC had on the younger kids.

The PDC want to hang up their coats and say they have been there and done it. There are kids looking up to them and they have made their changes at the right time. They are role models for the streets and it's great they are making the change now. We need to give them a chance.

Chapter Forty-one

Police

No one. None of the killings I've ever seen ever since I was a kid, never seen no one go down for a killing. Someone who is black and from the ghetto. Never seen no one convicted. Never. Never. The police think, 'Fuck that, he's a criminal.' They don't put the whole of their effort into the detective work because he's a criminal. Like, if I died now, the police aren't going to go potty and try and find my killers. All the grief I've given them over the years. They'd think 'Good.' That's what's happenin', innit? If it was a normal guy they'd put on their detective glasses and the CSI whole thing for a murder. Not with us, though.

JaJa

A few days after the shooting of Phat Si, JaJa received a letter from the police. They wanted information. They wanted anyone who knew something about the shooting to come forward. JaJa had no information. He wasn't there. But even if he did have information, going to the police was the last thing he would ever do. JaJa believed the police could never be trusted.

He remembered how a girl from Angell Town, not long ago, had been promised witness protection if she came forward and gave evidence about a shooting on Brixton Road. The case went to court. She testified, but then the case fell apart and the judge stopped the trial. The girl was now back in Brixton, unprotected, still on the streets.

That's so-called police protection. She ain't got no new house. That's dangerous. Can't do that. No way, you know what I'm saying. We know the police, we know what they are like. The police don't like you. You are a statistic. You are a piece of paperwork.

JaJa believed it was the same the world over. It was worldwide. Not just in Angell Town. All the PDC agreed with him. Bloods, Inch, Ribz, Maddix, Quinney all agreed that the police couldn't be trusted. Li'l Shak, one of the younger and more vocal PDC guys, had formed strong views from his nineteen years' experience of life on the estate.

They got their own crew. They're gang-bangers. The police are the biggest gang around here. They're around here more than anybody.

And Li'l Shak believed that the police were often responsible for further violence because they communicated the names of the chief suspects, via the local press, to the community.

The police don't help it because they'll come round here and if someone dies round here it's quicker for the police to call someone's name. When someone's name gets in the paper they go like, 'It's like an accident.' So automatically if someone dies and they say it's the PDC sometimes it's the police spreading some of them rumours and then it will lead back round to people and then vice versa and it doesn't help the situation. Sometimes you got the police playing more roles, making people die and making certain things happen in the community than the people in the community coz the system ain't trying to help it in certain ways.

The distrust ran so deep that JaJa wouldn't go to the police even if his younger brother Naja was shot.

I'd sort it out myself. That's the decision I take. That's the decision everyone takes. You know if you do something, you could go to prison for it. I'm not scared to take that risk. Last thing I think about is the police.

Chapter Forty-two

True Stories

The system just keeps a hold of you like, d'you get
me? You come out of jail, you've done your sentence
but you're still on licence for two years. Now what's
that about? And then in that two years it's so hard to
survive out here. You can't get a job coz of your
offences and so you're just going to do crime again
and then you're on licence again. It never stops.
True stories.

Bloods

By the end of 2006, there was relative peace in Angell Town. It was as though London needed some respite from the traumas of the terrorist bombings in July 2005 and the violence on its streets.

Gun crime statistics had begun to fall for the first time in two decades.

Bloods came out of prison and was amazed that JaJa had

achieved so much. The album and videos were out and being sold in record shops and by kids in Brixton High Street. JaJa was now talking about opening a string of barber shops and hair salons and getting into property to create a PDC business empire. Bloods was delighted to see that JaJa had put his entrepreneurial skills to use. He admired his business mind. *What for me is hard, is simple for him. I started PDC. But JaJa built it.*

Tempman was out of prison too. He'd been sent away for four months in the summer for robbery, common assault and possessing weed. He wondered whether the police had it in for him. He was angry with himself. He'd been taking it easy, living his life and chilling when he made the mistake of robbing a little kid of a watch. The kid told the police. *A black kid told the police. Eight months on remand because of this little punk.*

He was angry not so much that he'd been put away but because it was over a watch. A bloody watch.

While he was on remand he tried to get his head in order. Next time he wanted to do things differently. He wanted to be a changed man.

I just sat down for those months and sorted the shit that was going through my head. I needed to wise up and do things differently. I still had to find myself, who I was. That's what I was doing, finding out who I am. I didn't used to structure myself. I just used to run around and yell. That was it, really. I'm a reformed man. You need to go all the way up there, all the way back down and start again...

Inch was trying to 'make the future bright'. He found it hard to stay away from the distractions he'd grown up with. *The drugs and the temptations don't just go away.* Most of all he found it hard to settle. There was always the possibility of conflict in Angell Town.

> *Unless you squash it, it lingers. You can have a disagreement with someone and it won't go away. Things happen. You have an argument with someone and it carries on through the generations. Disputes carry on through the generations unless you squash anything that is lingering. I don't know if there is stuff lingering. Well, I do know, obviously. But I hope that it won't come up.*

He was trying to put an end to it, to concentrate on music, and on new ventures. With JaJa's help he had opened a hairdressing salon in Angell Town a few doors down from the music studio. Using the initials of the PDC they called it Prestige Designer Cuts. He'd managed to get a reduced rent for the premises by bargaining the leaseholders down to a good price. In spite of the improvements on the estate, the streets at the heart of Angell Town still had a reputation for trouble that put off the more commercially minded.

Inch's business just about managed to break even. It was no thanks to the local residents, though. It upset him that the best clients were not locals but people from outside Angell Town. Fortunately, when he'd started the business, he'd persuaded hairdressers from other salons outside the estate to come to work for him in Angell Town. The tactic had worked. It meant that his staff brought with them their best clients. It was what saved his salon. For some reason not many people in Angell Town would use Inch's salon. JaJa's mum and sisters would get their hair done there and a couple of girls he knew were also clients, but most people on the estate would bypass his salon and get their hair done in Lewisham or Peckham. Deep down he knew why he couldn't get locals to use the place.

Why? That's what I ask myself. If my girlfriend wanted her hair done I'd get it done in my mate's shop. But it don't always go like that. Let me give you an example. If you sell the best weed ever, the bredrens and the sly haters would rather travel and not buy it from you. 'Sly haters' — it means people who know you but they don't like you. There are some people like that from the estate. People don't like putting money into people's pockets they know. But if people choose to go past it and go to Streatham or elsewhere then that's their choice. I'm putting somewhere for them to use that's local. If they wish to use it they will. If they don't, they don't. I'm not going to cry about it.

He wanted to open a second branch, perhaps on the Brixton Road where there was more foot traffic. Expansion: that's what he wanted. It was like a 'spider leg' off from music, the main core of the PDC business. The plan was working but there were always money difficulties. There were all sorts of difficulties waiting out there in Angell Town.

It's a reality that mishaps happen. It slows me down. But now I try not to take it too personal like.

Recently Inch had suffered a serious setback. His younger brother Andrew, known on the streets as 'Biker', had been convicted of attempted murder. He'd shot a nightclub bouncer in Clapham during a night out. Biker had always claimed he didn't do it. A jury disagreed. Biker was a hyperactive, optimistic kid who always thought that life was going to turn out well. He thought he was going 'to bust case', in other words he thought he was going to get off. So when the judge gave him a seven-year prison sentence he was kind of shocked.

Sometimes Inch felt bad. Sometimes he felt that he had been a bad influence on his younger brother. Biker had followed in the footsteps of his older brother ever since they were two innocent young kids called Nathan and Andrew running around Angell Town. He'd followed him the first time the two of them met a young boy from Birmingham called Elijah in the Angell Town park. He'd followed him into drug dealing in the stairwells of Marston House. He'd followed him through juvenile prison. Inch worried that Biker had followed him into a life of crime.

If I'd been different maybe none of it would have happened. I can't think too much about it, though. At the end of the day, everyone has got their own brain.

He tried to make up for any guilty feelings by helping his brother through prison life. He tried to explain to him what it would be like in prison and the rollercoaster of emotions he would experience.

The hardest thing now was to dampen down Biker's expectations of what life would be like when he came out.

Inch knew that there would be a painful period of adjustment once the first flush of excitement at being out of prison faded away. He knew because it had happened to him.

Now he tried to be more realistic. But that didn't stop him dreaming that one day he and JaJa would turn the PDC into a business empire, with property, shops and music.

Along from Inch's hair salon, Birdie was now running the grocer's shop on the corner of Angell Town's main street with the help of his mum. He was still the only one who had managed to stay out of prison. It was a calculated move.

I know when to chill. I see things getting heated and I take a step back. I don't want to go to jail.

He was still living with the mother of his two kids, but they were going through a bad patch. Business at the shop was going OK but when there wasn't much money around there was always the temptation to get back on the streets and earn some easy money.

When I've got no money I'm all negative because I might be drawn in and do something wrong, coz people see the hunger in my face and might get me to do something I don't want to do. I don't want to go to jail. Everyone got their own mind. It's up to you.

But when he was feeling positive he could tap into his way of doing things, a tactic that had kept him out of prison all his life.

I can see past one way of getting tings, I can see multiple ways of doing tings. I sit there and try and analyse and get another way of doing tings. There was a point when I did one way. That's how I was getting money, but when there are no drugs around and there's a drought you have to do other tings…

Ribz had begun to get his life together. He was in a better state than he'd ever been before. He'd begun to lose some of the weight he'd put on since coming out of prison. He was now looking fit and had cut down on his dope smoking.

He was doing community work. When he'd last come out of jail he'd hooked up with a guy called Kolfi who had persuaded him to try and do some youth work. The two of them went to classes to learn about drugs, black history, family relationships, health and safety issues. Ribz managed to stick it out for a year, sitting in a classroom from 10 a.m. to 2 p.m. to get a qualification allowing him to work with kids. He passed his exam and was the proud owner of a youth worker's certificate. Since then he did the occasional piece of work on Lambeth youth projects. But recently he'd started slipping and had not turned up for some of the training exercises. The woman who ran it said he would have to repeat the training. That pissed Ribz off. The next day Ribz just decided not to turn up. He planned to take it up again soon, though. Once the music was running more smoothly and once he'd calmed down.

Sharon Kerr was running a child-minding business from her house now that JaJa had left home. She wanted to live in Jamaica eventually. Both her parents now lived there. She'd been out there to look at buying a plot of land in West Mullan, Runaway Bay or St Annes. But she didn't want to live like her parents. They'd both lived and worked in Britain for thirty years and got themselves a pension to buy a house each in Jamaica. At 6 p.m. in the evening, her mother would lock herself away in her house because of the crime. From behind the padlocked gates and shuttered windows, she'd natter on the phone to anyone who would listen about how great the Queen was and how the system in England was so much better than in Jamaica. Her father had inherited property but had never done anything with it. He'd never amounted to much. He just seemed to drink Jamaican rum all day long. For Sharon that was no way to live. Once she got to Jamaica she wouldn't live like that, doing nothing with the present and always hanging on to the past.

She still felt resentful towards them. Her father had kicked her out of the house when she was 14 and she had had to go and live in a squat. He'd tried to make it up to her in some sort of way by making sure he spoiled JaJa when he was young, but she'd never forgiven him for the way he had treated her.

That's why she made such an effort with her own kids. She was still prepared to defend JaJa. But she suffered for it. Recently she'd been driving her car when she heard a police siren. She pulled over and armed police got out.

'Get out the car. Get out the car.'

A police woman with forensic gloves searched her car. Then they said they would search her.

'Why?'

'We think you've got a gun on you. We think you or your son has been drug dealing.'

There was a scene.

Three policemen jumped on top of her, snapped her in handcuffs and took her to Brixton police station where they strip-searched her. They released her at five in the morning, without charge. But they fined her £80.

The police had even been to search her new house on the edge of Angell Town. She'd confronted them at the time.

'What for? Why you doing this?'

'We want to see the layout.'

It was nothing new for Sharon. She'd had a lifetime of what she called police harassment against her and her sons.

This is the police having a war with the kids. When they arrest these kids and the judge says have you got any evidence and they haven't, the kids get put back on the street, it's a vendetta.

Over the years she had got used to the way the police spoke to her and treated her. But she was aware that she had to watch what she was doing the whole time so as not to give the police any excuse. Whenever she or any of the family got in the car they knew they had to put their seatbelts on. *They'll stop us for anything.*

In spite of the police searches, JaJa had not been caught doing anything illegal. His biggest achievement that year had been staying out of prison like he'd sworn he would. He was trying to go straight, to concentrate on the music. The record label, PDC Entertainments Inc, was up and running but now he wanted to take it beyond the streets and up to the next level.

He wanted PDC Inc to become a national phenomenon, not just a local attraction. Then he dreamt of taking it to the international level. And he saw the potential, not just for PDC gang members, but for the next generation of kids growing up in Angell Town.

> *If someone like me succeeds, then all the little kids won't wanna be in a gang. They'll think gangs are boring. I'm trying. I'm the hope. They'll think, 'If he goes through the door, then …' They are living the gang life because they need to eat. I don't tell everybody to stop what they are doing. No. People have still gotta pay the bills, eat food and lead everyday life. Not everyone is gonna wait because JaJa is trying to do some good for us. That's not realistic.*

There was a limit to how much he could control what was going on with the younger kids on the estate.

> *I see kids with guns the whole time and I don't tell them to stop it. I say, 'Be careful.' That's all I can say. If a young guy comes to me and he's selling drugs or he wants to do robbery or something, there's only so much I can say. If someone steals a mobile phone I might be able to get it back and make the thief apologize but if it's sold on there's nothing I can do. I got no money. Tough luck. When I do break through, then I can say, 'Stop doing this.' Then we are talking business. But that's never happened on the streets before. The elders have never done that. That's why I need to go through that door.*

He now looked at the younger kids in the way that the 28s had looked at him when he was growing up. He saw the changes. He saw them grasping for their own identity. He saw them grasping for something new so that they could distinguish themselves from what had gone before.

The new generation was getting into 'colours'. It was the way the gangs acted in Los Angeles, with the Crips wearing blue and the Bloods wearing red. Now the PDC kids from Angell Town wore purple, the 'Loughborough Soldiers' from Loughborough Junction wore brown and the 'O.C.' gang from Myatt's Fields wore black. He knew the police were concerned about this latest craze among south London gang members and that they somehow regarded it as dangerously subversive, but to JaJa it was just history repeating itself. He remembered how, when he was young, one gang in Birmingham known as the Inch Eyes wore bandanas round their left ankles. To JaJa it was nothing new, just a way for young kids who didn't have much hope in their lives to gain a sense of importance and belonging.

The new generation comes through with something new. The younger ones always want something new. The next lot might say you can only wear Nike or Reebok. It's just a way of knowing who you are and who is who.

The new generation included his own kids. Three months earlier his girlfriend had given birth to a little boy. He was pleased. He also had another one on the way with another woman. He hadn't meant to have children, but he just didn't think carefully enough. He didn't use a condom. However, he was determined to look after them. He didn't want to be like his dad had been. He was already trying to think beyond gangs. *True stories*. It was a phrase the PDC used a lot. It meant 'for real'.

Chapter Forty-three

Return to Angell Town

I'm a grown man now. I can't go on wanting to be in a gang. Come on.

JaJa

It was spring 2007. It had been two years since I'd first met JaJa, Phat Si, Inch, Birdie, Bloods, Ribz and Tempman. During those two years I'd immersed myself in their gang life, met their mothers, brothers, sisters and friends, listened to their stories about guns, drugs and violence, and friends who'd been gunned down on the streets of Brixton. At first the stories about their street life had seemed random and meaningless but the longer I spent with them, the more their stories began to make some sort of sense.

I hadn't seen them for several weeks, but now I was back in Angell Town. Three young boys had just been shot dead near Brixton. The spotlight was once again on south London. I wanted to know how the shootings had affected the PDC. I wanted to know what had become of the seven young men who are at the heart of this story.

As I walked onto the estate a group of young black men ambled towards me past the brand new CCTV cameras and the estate's newly refurbished and freshly-painted houses. They were pushing a wheelchair. They were pushing Phat Si. He had been making a fast recovery considering the extent and severity of his injuries. He had been allowed out for the day from his rehabilitation hospital in Croydon and some of the PDC had brought him back to Angell Town. They were laughing and joking, visiting friends and old haunts, trying to gee him up for the months and years of hard work that would be needed to get his limbs moving again and his speech back.

Phat Si was the one who I'd always feared for. When I first met him he was tall, lean, muscly and vibrant, dressed in a black, tight-fitting vest with gold chains around his neck, drawing happily on a joint. Yet in spite of his physical strength and powerful presence he had always seemed to me to be the most vulnerable of the group. There was an unpredictable, violent energy about him which teetered on the brink of chaos. Maybe he'd predicted what would happen to him. Two years earlier he'd rapped on one of the videos.

> *'Prepare for the worst*
> *Coz all my life's been hexed and I'm living with a curse*
> *And I'm coming from the dirt, South West 9'*

Now, hunched in his wheelchair, he looked pale and confused. I held his good hand and asked him how he was. He responded with a half smile, a muffled noise and an ambiguous shake of the head. With that and a brief wave of the one hand he could still raise, he was wheeled off with his PDC mates laughing and joking into the heart of Angell Town. I remembered the last words he'd said to me before he'd got shot.

> *Hopefully, in a few years' time you know, I'll give you some more proper details. After this day there will be another life. Another twenty-five years to tell you about.*

Over the next few days I caught up with all of them.

Bloods was keeping his head down and trying to stay out of trouble. He'd moved to Birmingham for a while to keep away from the bad influences of Angell Town. He had to be careful. He'd been in prison so often that if he got into trouble again an even lengthier prison sentence awaited him.

Ribz had been badly affected by the shooting of Phat Si. He'd seen a lot of people get shot during his young life but because it was one of his own 'bredren' it had touched him much more. He couldn't spend too much time thinking about it because he just ended up in tears. To shake himself out of his gloom he came up with an explanation. It was a hard, streetwise explanation. It was the only explanation he had.

> *But shit happens, that's how it goes, innit, living the life we live? If you are involved, if you are around people that are involved in things, you're gonna be a target, innit? You gotta expect shit to happen. Thank the Lord that he's still alive, d'you get me? It could have been worse.*

He felt bad, though, when he saw Phat Si being wheeled around

Angell Town. He felt bad because he couldn't just click his fingers and make him better. He felt bad that he didn't know what to say to him. He felt bad that the friend who used to prowl around Angell Town as one of the gang was now in hospital. He felt bad because seeing him was a constant reminder that anything can happen. *You could be in the wrong place at the wrong time and it would all be over.*

It was Islam that kept him going. That's where Ribz found hope. Through Islam he was just trying to make every day better than the day before, to keep things positive.

There's more than banging guns, being on the road, linking girls, raving, hanging around a bag of people who don't give a fuck about you. Life's bigger than that.

His new serious outlook on life was one reason why he'd started to try and track down his father again. He still didn't know much about him. First he'd heard that he was in America. A few months before that someone had told him they'd just seen him in Jamaica. Everybody he tried to contact to find out where he was gave him different information. It was becoming more and more important for him to find his dad so that he could work out which women on the estate were his sisters. He was still worried about falling for a girl and finding out later that she was his sister.

I don't need to see my dad. He ain't got nuffin' to say to me. But I would like to find him obviously and go through certain things. I don't know what I'd ask him. It's my family, innit? That's the main concern for me because I don't like to be out there and talking to my sister because, d'you get me, that's not right. So I know I've got a lot of sisters on the estate, from his side, from my father's side, so that's why I want to find. And I think I can find out.

He still found it difficult to get on with his mum. She was now 46, out of prison and living in a flat down the road in West Norwood with his two sisters. Since she'd last got out of prison she'd stopped taking hard drugs, like crack and heroin, but was still drinking too much alcohol. He tried to see her every week but it was painful. They argued the whole time. If he took the side of someone who disagreed with her she would get upset.

'You hate me, don't you?'

Ribz didn't mean to rise to the provocation. It was just that if he thought someone else was in the right he felt he had to say so. But that just got her even more worked up.

'You always take other people's sides. You hate me. You hate me because you think I abandoned you.'

He didn't have an answer to that.

He'd tried living with his mum for a couple of weeks. He thought that it might make them closer after all the years they'd spent apart. But it didn't work out. The clashes were just too stormy. His relationship with her hadn't changed. He doubted it ever would. At least now she was off the crack.

He was finally getting on better with his older brother, Skippy. Skippy, like his mother, had also managed to get off the crack. Ribz believed it was prison that had helped his brother and his mum. Although Ribz hated everything about prison he recognized it had saved them. It was being locked up that had finally broken their crack addiction.

His brother was in Birmingham, keeping fit and training to

be an athletics coach. Ribz could hardly believe it. A couple of years earlier, when his brother was a crackhead, Ribz would have done anything to avoid bumping into him. Now, although they didn't see much of each other, they were at least getting on. That was the power of family.

Things hadn't gone so well for his 'other' family, the foster family where he'd spent a miserable youth being hit and smacked by the woman who ran the home. He'd recently bumped into the woman's daughter who he'd suspected of dealing drugs from the front gate of the house when he was growing up. She'd been skulking around Angell Town looking older, haggard and defeated.

If you'd seen her before you would never believe it. She used to have everything, all glamorous, nice gold earrings, nice braids, all suited and booted. Now she's messed up on hard drugs.

And that was Ribz's greatest achievement. He'd stayed off drugs and out of trouble. The only problem he'd had with the police had been a couple of months before. He'd been walking his mum's pit bull terrier in West Norwood when a police officer had come up to him. He said that they had a description of a dog being involved in a dog fight and that Ribz's pit bull matched that description. The policeman asked for his details, but Ribz refused to give them. Then, when the policeman turned nasty, Ribz gave a false name.

The officer stared him down.

'I know that's not your name. I've watched you grow up since you were little.'

'I don't know what you are talking about.'

'We used to raid your house when you were a kid. So come on, tell me your real name.'

That brought home to Ribz just how much he'd been in trouble and how infamous he was with the local police. He thought it was mad that the police could still remember him from when he was a little kid.

He decided it was best to give his real name.

In the end, it wasn't his mum's dog that had been involved in the dog fight after all. Nevertheless the incident with the police officer was another wake-up call. It was a reminder to Ribz of just how much of his life had revolved around crime. He was determined that the rest of his life would follow a different path.

Birdie was still trying to make tunes. He'd given up producing beats and had now started 'spitting' or rapping. He was bringing out music under his own name rather than under the name of the PDC. He thought that it wouldn't harm the PDC label. He thought that competition between them was good for business and would help everyone up their game.

Out of all the PDC Birdie was the only one who had managed to stay out of prison. He was still in the clear, just as he'd promised all those years earlier. He had complaints but he lived a life that seemed more stable than the others. He ran the grocery shop down the road from the Angell Town recording studio, made his music, stayed out of trouble and looked after his two kids and their mother. In spite of the stress of family life and the difficulties he'd recently been having with his partner he hoped his relationship with her would last. *But who knows what the future holds?*

Tempman believed he was a reformed man. He'd made a decision to stay away from the 'Muslim Boys' because it was getting too heavy. Police had rounded up most of the ringleaders and put them in jail. A few months earlier Tempman watched those associated with the gang collapse under internal disputes.

They said they were Muslims but still people robbed and got drunk and started slipping. There were ten leaders in the room and they are going to fight each other and each want to do their own ting. There was fights and arguments and that's what happened. D'you get me G?

He had a young kid on the way and he was trying to settle down. He was still only 19 but he believed he was ready for the new challenge.

I'm very happy. I got enough money to buy food to put in the fridge to look after my young buck and my woman. I'm a reformed man now. I gotta do that.

Drawing heavily on a joint he talked about his remaining task. He was going to track down his father. He didn't know where he was, or what he looked like. He just knew his name was Paul.

I hadn't seen Inch for several months. He'd been in prison, serving a six months' prison sentence, but now he was out again. Ironically, after all the serious crime he'd been involved in, what sent him back to prison was a driving licence offence.

It had happened in late February. The month was significant.

For Inch it explained why he'd been targeted for such a minor act. During two mad February weeks in south London, three teenage boys had been shot dead, including 15-year-old Billy Cox, gunned down on Valentine's Day in his house in Clapham, just down the road from Angell Town. Inch thought that the media outcry following the shootings was responsible for what happened to him.

He'd been near Brixton, sitting behind the steering wheel of a stationary car waiting for someone. In the rear-view mirror he saw a police car pull up behind him. His heart beat faster and he began to sweat. It was a familiar feeling whenever the police approached him. The police tapped on the car window and asked him to get out of the car. He was taken to Brixton police station and asked to show his licence. He didn't have one. He knew the police knew that. He'd never passed his test.

He spent the night in a cell and the next day he appeared in front of a judge. She listened to the evidence. Inch pleaded guilty.

Inch wasn't too worried. He thought, at worst, he would get community service. So when the judge spoke up he was confused.

'You're getting a six-month sentence.'

Inch stood in the dock, not understanding. He looked at his solicitor.

'What did she say? What did she just say?'

His solicitor looked back at him as they took him away.

'I'll come down and see you.'

'No, what did she just say? Tell me now. What did she say? Am I going home?'

Six months. He thought it was a six month community service order. Or perhaps an order saying that he had to stay out of trouble for six months.

I really thought I was going home. If I'd had the slightest thought I was going to jail I wouldn't have been in that car. Elijah hasn't got jailed for anything. Other friends who are on the road don't get anything and I get six months' jail just like that.

His solicitor spoke to him when he was in the court cells.

'We are going to appeal.'

That's when it sunk in. That's when he knew for sure that he wasn't going home. He was going back to prison for six months.

'Fuck it.'

Inch banged the cell door and got his head ready for the prison sentence ahead of him.

He tried not to take it personally.

I thought it's nothing. I've done more than that on the block so I'm not going to do any different, it's not going to make me change. It's just going to piss me off for those long months ahead. I was stupid to be in the car. You have to accept it.

He knew he'd have to serve at least three months. It would have been bearable if it wasn't for the fact that being back in prison was like going back to an old school he'd left years ago. He felt silly being there, back with people who had no ambition and who were feeling fucked up. He felt old. There were kids bragging about guns and what they were involved in. Inch felt he'd moved on. Now he just wanted to do his time and go home.

That's when the police came calling. Detectives came to his cell and started questioning him about the shootings in South London.

They wanted to know about 15-year-old Billy Cox and why he was shot dead.

'Listen, your friends are talking to us, so why don't you? Your friends are helping us with enquiries.'

'I've nothing to help you with. I don't know these little kids and if I did know them I wouldn't be trying to kill them. I know nothing about no Billy.'

As soon as I got to jail they were talking about the gang boss thing and putting known gang bosses into jail. The police checked on me every week and they wanted to know about things happening in our area and why are little kids getting involved in guns. I don't know why they would be trying to scare me. They wanted to find out, or match up, or I don't know what the fuck they were doing. They just wanted to get me off the roads, innit?

The prison sentence gave him yet more time to think. He knew that the judge had probably given him a longer sentence because of the media hysteria over the south London shootings. He knew the police were just looking for any excuse to put him away. He knew it was stupid to get caught like that, over something so trivial. But sometimes he felt that he was trapped in a vicious circle. He needed money, but he didn't have cash to get a cab so he had to borrow a car, which was how he was caught. He believed that hindsight, for people in his situation, was a luxury.

Obviously when things happen in reality, they just happen. I was thinking about my mistake. I was thinking about it in prison every day but sometimes things just happen and that's when you can do nothing about it. Sometimes you can and that's when you can run. Other times you just get caught.

When he was released there was no big homecoming party. He'd not been gone long. But he was home. That was the main thing. He spent the day playing with his daughter, who was now two years old. He'd missed her. *She's the best thing ever. She's proper. I love her.*

At the end of the day, though, he wasn't bitter about being put in prison. He'd driven loads of times and had always got away with it. *I haven't been no angel when it comes to driving.* But out of all the times he'd been out driving, he'd been caught when he was sitting in a stationary car. That was odd.

Maybe, he thought, it was time to apply for a driving test.

I stopped off to see Sharon Kerr. She was sitting with her daughter Chantelle in their modern, newly built house on the edge of Angell Town. She hadn't been speaking to JaJa. They'd had an argument a few weeks back.

She knew that he had calmed down since he'd last been back to prison and that he'd stayed out of jail. But she saw the pressure mounting on him. She saw the bills he had to pay, the rent on his flat and office, the two kids with different mothers he had to look after. He seemed to be coping OK with staying straight, but she didn't know how long he was going to last.

She confronted him one day.

'Why don't you go out and get a job as a cleaner or something?' He wouldn't listen.

She hoped history wouldn't repeat itself because it was hard on all the family when he was locked up. The time and money spent trekking around the country visiting him in different jails was exhausting. She didn't want to do it any more. Her eldest son had caused her a lifetime of worry.

Since Elijah turned 18, I have been expecting the door to knock and someone to tell me he's been shot, so I'm kind of reserved on that. I'm just waiting now if you know what I mean.

Chantelle, Sharon's daughter and Elijah's sister, believed it wasn't going to be easy for anyone who decided to take on her brother. It was his connections, she believed, that would keep him safe.

It's just that it's a big thing. Then if you are going to do that, then you have to watch your own back, you have to think about it. You can't just go and shoot Elijah. It's a big thing. He knew so much people, he's got so much family and we haven't even got a big family but we know a lot of people and it's a big thing. It will be a scene and the person will have to think about it carefully because it won't be a small matter. They would have to be careful because we are a different set of people.

Sharon thought back on her story. She thought back on her long journey from Birmingham to Tulse Hill. She thought back on the move from Streatham to Angell Town and all those hard years spent on the estate. *In the end it's made us stronger. But I am tired.*

I walked back through Angell Town to the place JaJa used as his office. Piles of CDs and DVDs took up the shelves. Posters of PDC events and music lined the walls. One of the posters was of the PDC taken years ago. Phat Si, Inch, JaJa, Bloods, Maddix, Li'l Shak, Tiny, Birdie and Ribz were all in it, making hard, gang poses, but looking fresh, vibrant and energetic. JaJa stood and stared at it.

'That there poster tells a lot of stories.'

To most people, the office, with its racks full of CDs and DVDs and its posters on the wall announcing new PDC events, wouldn't look much. But at that moment I saw it as a huge achievement. It was a reminder of just how far they'd come. JaJa had grown up looking at drug dealers and thieves, arguing, robbing, stabbing and shooting each other outside the kitchen window of his council block. Most of the others had grown up alone on the streets or watching their mothers and brothers disappear into a dazed, crack-fuelled fog.

A television was burbling away in the corner of the room. It was a news item on the latest spate of gun and knife crime that had hit the capital. In the previous week there had been four fatal stabbings. The man being interviewed was saying that he was going to wage war on street gangs and that tackling gun and knife culture was a priority for the coming year. JaJa looked up.

'Who's that white man on television?'

'That's Sir Ian Blair, the chief of the Metropolitan Police.'

'He's talking rubbish.'

JaJa was furious that he was still being stopped by police at least once a week.

Each time it was the same routine.

'Freeze. Get down.'

'You're not going to find anything on me.'

'You got a gun on you today. Where's your gun?'

'You know I ain't got a gun.'

The police would just laugh at him. It was like a game to them. They taunted him.

'I hear you are trying to go straight. We're still going to get you.'

Now what he did every time it happened was text his solicitor. He reckoned he got stopped randomly at least once a week.

As Sir Ian Blair burbled in the background about next year's tough new policing methods, JaJa launched into the last story he ever told me, a story set in the future.

Chapter Forty-four

Goodbye to Angell Town

It's not that I hate England. It's the ghetto. It's the street life I want to get away from. Twenty-five years of street life is too much stress. Why do I have to live like this? It pisses me off. People might say, 'You shouldn't do a life of crime, you should work 9 to 5.' Well, my life didn't go that way and it's come to this. I could see one road only and that is crime. Years ago, like I told you, the only people I could talk to were the criminals outside my window. There's people worse off than me, with no mum or dads and that. Who do they turn to? They turn to the street.

JaJa

JaJa didn't want to stay in Angell Town. Even though the estate was being touted as one of the success stories of inner-city regeneration JaJa couldn't really see the progress. Sometimes he would watch coaches draw up outside Angell Town and disgorge groups of besuited civil servants, architects and do-gooders from all over Europe who had come to look round the 'flagship' estate, a blueprint for what could apparently be done with 'inner-city problem areas.' In spite of the new architecture and sparkling street furniture, JaJa still saw it as a 'ghetto' from which he wanted to escape. *There is a whole world out there and I have to get out.* There were too many temptations in Angell Town. He was so used to getting easy money that every time he stepped into a shop and saw an open till, his hands started itching.

I've been in a bank and had to turn round and walk out so it doesn't look as though I'm looking round and that. It happens to me every day. That's how it is. It's quick temptations, though. If you overpower those you will be all right.

He just needed to have enough money to put food in his cupboard, pay his bills and help feed his two kids. His two sons were a year old and six months old. They were living with their respective mothers. He now took the older one on Friday and Saturday but preferred to leave the younger one with her mother. He wasn't too good at dealing with it when his baby boy started crying.

But he saw a future for them. He saw a future for them that was better than the future he had faced growing up.

Our parents went through a lot of hardship but they didn't manage to change things but we are trying to change things and the younger ones have more access. When I was young I used to like dancing. I used to love dancing. I used to win dancing competitions. I wanted to be an actor but as a kid that got wiped out. I thought no one is going to let me do that. No one will help me through that. You learn that you can't do what you want to do. You get it in your head you have to do what everyone else does so you become a drug dealer, or a gangster. But kids today have much more choices and I'm gonna say to my son that he can be an actor. I'm gonna let him do karate and boxing. That's giving him choices. If you have a choice there'll be more options open to you.

He saw a better future for his kids, but also for his friends. He saw PDC Inc as an international record label that would launch the artistic careers of Inch, Birdie, Ribz, Bloods and Tempman.

And after the latest news from the hospital in Croydon, he saw a better future for Phat Si.

A few days before, without telling anyone, Phat Si had wheeled himself out of the hospital grounds towards a bus stop on the London Road which was right outside the hospital entrance. Then he had slid himself out of the chair, hauled himself to his feet, clung onto the bus stop and waited.

When the number 109 bus to Brixton arrived, he pulled himself up the steps, paid for a ticket, and collapsed onto the nearest seat. An hour later, when he got to his destination, he lowered himself off the bus, walked five steps and collapsed exhausted onto a wall. Then he took out his mobile phone and rang round some of his friends. Because he couldn't make himself understood he just grunted at their questions. Then he called Janelle, the mother of his kid.

When Janelle answered Phat Si's call she was confused. She heard the sound of traffic in the background. But he was supposed to be in hospital.

'Simon, where are you? Tell me where you are.'

Phat Si grunted. He still couldn't string words together.

'Put the phone on speaker.'

He did as he was told.

She shouted into the phone.

'Hello. Is anyone there? If someone is out there can you take the phone off him?'

A passer-by saw Phat Si holding up the phone and took it.

Over the phone, Janelle explained to the surprised pedestrian that the man he had taken the phone from was supposed to be in hospital and that he had difficulty talking. She wanted to know whether he could tell her where he was.

The man gave her the name of a street in Stockwell.

Phat Si had ended up outside his old home on the Stockwell Park Estate.

When his friends came for him they found Phat Si in his G Star jacket, his G Star jeans falling off his bum, propped up on a wall in Stockwell, tired but defiant. He was outside the house he had grown up in, the house his mother had abandoned when he was eight years old.

It turned out that he had wanted one of his friends to come and pick him up and take him out of the hospital. When no one came he had decided to make the journey himself. It was what he had always done. He had looked after himself ever since he was an eight-year-old kid.

When JaJa was told the story of Phat Si's solo journey to Stockwell he was pleased. It showed that once again he was ready to take on the world as he'd had to do all his life. There was triumph in that short journey.

It shows he's getting better. It shows he's more like his old self. It's good news.

JaJa too had experienced his own small triumphs. Even though JaJa had money difficulties, he had never gone back to prison. He was so used to getting red bills that when a white one arrived it was a pleasant surprise. BT often phoned to chase him up.

'I ain't got no money.'

'OK.'

They didn't seem to worry about his unpaid bills so he didn't either.

To stop himself from getting depressed he looked forward to the day, some time in the future, when he'd made it big so that he could get away and live in another country. He'd give his mum some money so that she could live anywhere she liked.

If I don't die I'm going to say goodbye to Angell Town and live somewhere else. But I'd come back to Angell Town to say hello to everyone, now and again. I'm going to get out. If we blow and get big, I'm off. I'll come and visit and remember how I used to live in Angell Town.

He fantasized about coming back one day to see the people and places he grew up around. He would nod at neighbours as he walked by.

'How ya doing? Still living in Fairweather Road?'

That's the sort of thing he'd say to people who still lived there. He'd come back and remember what it was like and how it used to be. After all, Angell Town had helped him. Angell Town had formed him. That's why he had PDC tattooed on his neck. *Because it's for life.* He would never forget where he came from. But if he stayed in Angell Town that would be too much. He might be shot. Anything might happen.

I'd be upset if I died in Angell Town. That's the worst. Getting shot and dying, to go all this time and die in Angell Town, that's the worst thing that could happen.

But it was a reality. The reality was that some people in Angell Town were mad and unpredictable.

Every time I walk out my house I'm at risk. Someone who thinks I'm responsible for shooting someone might come after me. It could be his sisters or uncles or cousins or aunties. It could be anyone who decides to retaliate. It could be to revenge a death. It could be something stupid like imagining a disrespect. That's all it takes. That's how it is now. I could die right now.

The latest scare had happened a couple of days before. He'd been walking through Brixton when he saw out of the corner of his eye a car with tinted windows slow down and draw up alongside him. The window wound down. JaJa had thought that this was the end.

I thought this was it and I thought is this going to happen now? I shouldn't think like that but it shows how I think. The thing is that I'm not scared. That's what scared me. That I'm not scared. If someone walks too close behind me I always think what's going to happen. That's how most of my friends think. That's how it's affecting us.

Anything could set him thinking like that. Strange noises in his house at night would get him worried. He knew that he had to get out of there and move on with his life. He'd had enough. But the only way out of the cycle and towards a healthy and happy future was to take each day as it comes. And each day he had to stop himself from being tempted back to easy money, guns, drugs, life on the streets. And no one could help him. Not the police, not his mum. Not even the PDC. *Slowly but surely.* That was his motto now.

Epilogue

JaJa, real name Elijah Kerr, is now 27 years old. He is still concentrating on music and pursuing his goal of building the biggest independent record label in the UK. He has just had a baby daughter and is enjoying being the father of three young kids. He still lives in Angell Town.

Phat Si, real name Simon Maitland, is 27 years old. He is recovering from gunshot wounds to the head and is beginning to regain some speech. He is now out of hospital and lives near Angell Town.

Bloods is 27 years old and has moved to Birmingham in an attempt to stay away from the troubles in Angell Town.

Inch, real name Nathan Cross, is 26 years old. He is trying to open a second hairdressing salon and is living happily with his daughter and her mother in Angell Town.

Birdie, real name Michael Deans, is 26 years old. He lives with his partner and their two children in Angell Town where he runs the small local supermarket. He is trying to build a music career as a solo artist.

Ribz, real name Byron Cole, is 24 years old. He is working with Lambeth Youth Projects and has two children. He lives near Angell Town. He still has not been able to track down his father.

Tempman, real name Darren Samuels, is 19 years old. He is doing youth work and is trying to build up his own record label, Southside Records. He lives near Angell Town. He has become a father for the first time and is still searching for his own father.

Sharon Kerr is working as a child-minder and is buying a plot of land to build her retirement home in Jamaica. She lives one street away from Angell Town.

Chantelle Kerr is mother to two children and lives next to Angell Town.

Pod, now known as Roger Samuels, is a pastor and professional gospel singer who performs all around the world. He lives in Croydon with his wife and four kids.

Naja, JaJa's younger brother, Li'l Shak, Sykes, Quinney, Tiny and Maddix, with the help of Earl Myers, are working on new music tracks in the Angell Town studio.

Skippy, Ribz's brother, is in Birmingham, training to be an athletics coach.

K Nutz is serving time for armed robbery.

Biker, Inch's younger brother, hopes to be released from prison soon, having served over half of his seven-year sentence for firearms offences and attempted murder.

Afterword

by Elijah Kerr (JaJa)

You've read our story. It's a story of real pain. You've read things about me and Phat Si and my friends growing up together and how it can end. Some of us are dead. Some of us nearly died. Most of us went to jail. You can see that when we were growing up it wasn't just a phase that we jumped into, a phase that came out of the blue.

We are not saying that we blame society for what went wrong. We admit we made mistakes. We are normal kids that made mistakes. I made loads of mistakes.

What I'm saying is that when I wanted to go on the straight and narrow there wasn't much support. When the young kids go bad, do crime, go to jail and finally realize there's more to life than guns and drugs, where do they go for support? Who is there for them? It's just us against the world.

We need help. Please help us.